SHEFFIELD CRIMES

SHEFFIELD CRIMES

A Gruesome Selection of Victorian Cases

MARGARET DRINKALL

The
History
Press

First published 2011

The History Press
The Mill, Brimscombe Port
Stroud, Gloucestershire, GL5 2QG
www.thehistorypress.co.uk

British Library Cataloguing in Publication Data.
A catalogue record for this book is available from the British Library.

ISBN 978 0 7524 5820 5

Typesetting and origination by The History Press
Manufacturing managed by Jellyfish Print Solutions Ltd.
Printed in India

CONTENTS

ACKNOWLEDGEMENTS

This book continues to explore the fascination I have with true murder and crime in the Victorian period. It does not focus purely on murder and manslaughter, but also includes other crimes which were committed during the years between 1837 and 1880. This selection of crimes gives a better understanding of the lives of the criminal element of Sheffield. All of the crimes in this book were committed by real people who, naturally, wished to evade the law – and I have no doubt that many others actually succeeded. The Sheffield police force in these early days operated with largely unsophisticated methods. The city during the Victorian period was expanding and reaching out towards what used to be little villages surrounding the town. Many of its districts were unhealthy and unclean, places where vast numbers of people lived out their lives in overcrowded slums. But not all crimes were committed by brutish and cunning citizens. In these pages you will find crimes committed by sextons, nurses and doctors, as well as by the ordinary people of the town.

The reporters who wrote about these crimes did not always get names and places correct, and in some instances I have had to use my own initiative. Any mistakes are therefore my own. It was usual that an inquest would be held following the finding of a body, to establish the cause of death. It usually took place in the nearest public house. The jury was able to inspect the body before the inquest and, if their verdict was a guilty one, the suspect would be sent for trial at the Assizes. These Assizes, which were held at Leeds and York on a quarterly basis, were where the felons would receive their sentence. This could be anything from a few years' imprisonment, sometimes with hard labour, to transportation for life, depending on the severity of the case.

As always, the production of a book is a team effort and I would like to thank the team at The History Press for their help. I would also like to thank the Sheffield Local Studies Department for all the illustrations in the book from their collection of 'Picture Sheffield'. I am ever grateful for the support and help of my family and friends, such as Ruth Peattie, Ali Bloy and Yvonne Mitcheson for their continued encouragement. I would also like to extend my gratitude to you, the people who buy this book, as without you none of this would be possible.

Chapter One

 BODYSNATCHING AT HILLSBOROUGH

The criminal element of Sheffield was capable of devising many opportunities for making money. No crime was considered too small – or indeed too horrendous. At the time, 'bodysnatching' (entering graveyards in the middle of the night to disinter bodies which had been recently buried) was perceived as one of the most heinous types of crime; the bodies so removed were then sold to medical schools for dissection. The Edinburgh resurrectionists Burke and Hare had become famous for their bodysnatching in January 1829: in order to ensure that fresh bodies were available, they took the lives of some of the victims themselves (coining the phrase 'burking', meaning 'to murder for sale', in the process). After a lengthy trial, Burke was hanged; Hare, however, was released, having given evidence against his accomplice. The populace of the city was so incensed by the crime that, following the trial, Hare was forced to flee Edinburgh – lynch mobs were after him. Bereaved relatives attempted to protect the corpses of recently deceased family members from this awful fate by standing guard over the grave until decomposition had set in, rendering the corpse useless to the medical schools. Some erected cages over the site of the grave itself. The opprobrium surrounding these crimes was such that most resurrectionists, when caught, went in fear of their lives.

The fear that any person could be the subject of dissection was felt so deeply in Sheffield that the medical school, built in 1826, was burned down by a mob in 1835. In Sheffield, all paupers whose bodies lay unclaimed could be offered to the medical school for dissection: therefore there was no need to 'burke' anyone, as the supply of bodies from the workhouse paupers was said to be 'ample'. But still the fear did not go away. Thirty-six years later, when rumours began to circulate that a Sheffield sexton had been selling bodies to the new medical school, it was enough to incite the mob to violence.

The sexton's name was Isaac Howard, and he lived in a house built by himself at the burial ground of St Phillip's Church at Hillsborough. He was very proud of his house, which was built of stone, two storeys tall and had five or six rooms. It was described as 'a very comfortable working-class residence'. In March of 1862 he invited gravedigger Robert Dixon and his wife to become lodgers, and they

Sheffield Medical School (nearest to camera).

The Dissecting Room, Sheffield Medical School.

moved in on the 24th of the month. It didn't bother the Dixons that they lived so close to the cemetery, as that was where Mr Dixon made his living. They were happy with the bedroom, which was over the stable. The only problem was the smell. When Dixon mentioned it to Howard he brushed it off, saying that 'it often happens,' but not to worry, as 'it will go away'. The smell did not go away: in fact, it got worse. Dixon, investigating the source of the smell, went to the door of the stable, but found it was locked. He made a hole in the floor of his bedroom and looked through into the stable below.

The sight that greeted him was one which he would never forget: beneath him lay at least twenty coffins, filled with the remains of bodies of different sexes and ages – ranging from teenagers of about fifteen or sixteen years to stillborn babies. The coffins did not have lids on or any kind of covering and were piled up one on top of each other. Dixon, horror-struck, started to watch Howard more closely. He noted that Howard kept the key to the stables hidden, and he often saw him coming and going. On another occasion, once again peeping through the hole in the floor, he saw the body of a child. He once more complained about the smell, and this time Howard moved the body out of the stable and put it into a shed. Dixon also noted that two other men often went into the stables and the nearby shed, under the direction of Howard. Peering from his bedroom window one day, he saw him put the body of the child onto a barrow, along with two other bodies – one a boy of ten and another body of fifteen years old – and take them away.

A few weeks later Dixon found the stable door unlocked. Seizing his opportunity, he went inside and saw yet another group of coffins. This time there were about twenty of them. There was also a pile of thirty nameplates that had been unscrewed from coffins, which he took to show his employer, Mr Oxspring. Oxspring immediately took the nameplates to the Chief Constable of Sheffield, Mr John Jackson. Before the Chief Constable could act, however, rumours began to fly around the town that a local sexton had been selling bodies to the medical school. Despite the fact that only the freshest corpses were suitable for dissection, the rumours gained credence, for the porter of the Sheffield Medical School was a regular visitor to Howard's cemetery…

Hundreds of people flocked to the cemetery at Hillsborough on Tuesday 3 June, shouting for Howard to come out of his house and face them. When Howard did not appear, threats were made upon his life. By afternoon the crowd had increased and the police were brought in, but they were powerless to stop such a large group. By teatime there was pandemonium – and the enraged crowd had decided to set fire to Howard's house. The door was kicked in and the crowd poured inside. The only occupant was Mrs Howard, who was clearly terrified. Ignoring her cries to stop, men piled the furniture in the middle of the room and set it on fire. By midnight the house was a gutted shell. The Sheffield Fire Brigade was called out, but due to the

Above left: Chief Constable Mr John Jackson.

Above right: Sheffield Fire Brigade with a horse-drawn fire engine.

ferocity of the fire, which had quickly taken hold, little could be done. Several people stated, quite loudly, that if Howard had been there he would have been thrown bodily onto the flames. The next day, the Chief Constable arrived at the cemetery to examine the remains of the house. As Howard was still nowhere to be seen, Mr Jackson investigated the cemetery, and found a large hole at the side of a hilly piece of ground where several coffins lay exposed. The stench was appalling. Dixon told him his story, and Mr Jackson went into the stables. Inside he found a box containing the dissected body of a man. Obtaining a larger box and putting the smaller box holding the remains inside, he immediately took it to the Town Hall. It was decided, because of the riot and the questions that were being asked, that an inquiry needed to be held.

It was held at the Town Hall on 14 June 1862 before the magistrates. Mr Howard was summoned to appear, but he did not attend (in fear of his life, it was believed). However, he did appoint a solicitor to take out a peace warrant against Robert Dixon; the magistrates dismissed the solicitor and the warrant, as it could only be put into effect if Howard had attended in person. The aptly named Mr Skinner, who was a lecturer at the medical school, emphasised that the school had a licence from the Secretary of State to hold dissections by the students of anatomy. He identified the remains of the body Mr Jackson had discovered in the stable as those of fifty-six-year-old Joseph Greatorex, who had died of bronchitis on 6 May at the Sheffield Workhouse. It was the practice that the workhouse master would notify the sexton of deaths in the workhouse; the sexton would then collect the body, and a certificate from the workhouse doctor stating the cause of death, and deliver both to the medical school (where he could claim a fee of 5s). On completion of the dissection, the remains would be handed back to the sexton and given for burial to the incumbent of St Phillip's, Revd John Livesey, who would then issue a certificate stating that the remains had been buried with all the burial rites. Mr Skinner told the inquiry that he recognised the remains of the body as he had been using it in his lectures to the students for the past month. The magistrates demanded to know how many bodies had been delivered to the medical school for dissection. Another doctor, Mr Barber, told them that there had been ten bodies from October to March 1862, and all the bodies had been brought from the workhouse. He explained that the supply of bodies being ample, the medical school had no cause to seek bodies anywhere else. On the contrary, he pointed out, if they had needed more they could have doubled that amount from the workhouse.

The inquiry then looked at why the dissected remains had still been above ground and not buried decently, and an even more dubious practice came to light. The Revd Livesey told the magistrates that there had not been a burial service for the dissected remains, and that it was not a legal requirement to hold one: the Burial Act only stated that the body had to be 'decently interred in consecrated grounds'. The magistrates stated their disgust at such a procedure – that any person, whether a pauper or not, should not receive a proper Christian burial service was a disgrace.

Revd Livesey, in an attempt to defend himself, wrote to the local newspaper the following week placing the blame for the debacle squarely on Howard's shoulders. He stated that Howard had been a sexton for thirty years and had advised him as to the procedure for dealing with bodies from the workhouse. 'How could I read a service over a mass of putrid matter in a wooden box in a most offensive state?' he asked. 'It would have been indecent to do it. If the body had been in a proper coffin or in a shell, I would have been delighted for it to be done.'

This in turn brought to light the disrespectful way in which the remains had been transported. They were brought to the medical school by the sexton in a sack, and after dissection were hastily pushed into a wooden box for interment. The magistrates, to the discomfiture of the reverend, then produced a signed certificate stating that Revd Livesey had held a burial service over the body. The certificate mentioned the service, clearly stating 'by whom performed' – a space which the reverend had signed with a flourish. At that time, of course, the body

Entrance Gates and Lodge, Sheffield Workhouse.

was still in a box in the stable, a fact of which the reverend was well aware. The magistrates pointed out to him that there were only three times when a burial service could be refused: when the deceased had been excommunicated; where the deceased had not been baptised; or where a coroner had reached a decision of *felo de se* – an old legal term for suicide. Livesey was clearly shocked when the magistrates told him that he had in fact committed a crime, and that he was to be charged with making a false entry on a legal document and would have to go to trial at the Assizes. When Livesey was asked how he pleaded to the charge, he said that he would reserve his defence for the trial. The crowd which had assembled outside the Town Hall, enraged at the entire affair, hooted at Livesey as he left the court. The inquiry closed without any resolution to the case, as Howard had still not appeared to give evidence. A warrant was issued for his arrest.

The feelings in the town were such that the following Sunday, 15 June, even more people assembled at St Phillip's churchyard. A local reporter was there to record the events, and he stated that some members of the crowd were armed with picks and shovels – they intended to dig up the graves of their relatives to find out if the bodies had been tampered with. Feelings still ran very high. One of the crowd told the reporter that she was the mother of a child buried eight months previously: her little boy, Edwin Charles Shearsmith, had been two years and one month old when he died. The funeral had been held on 23 September 1861 and she had paid 10s to the sexton for digging the grave. She told the reporter that she had noted at the time that not much earth had been put on the grave. (Howard, with an eye to the main chance, had even told her that for the payment of a further 22s he could reserve the plot as a family grave.) Several coffins were now dug up, and amongst the bodies brought to light she claimed to recognise the features of her son. In a gruesome turn of events, she refused to leave the remains at the cemetery. Instead, she took the body of the child home with her. Mrs Shearsmith told the reporter that other women had done the same with their departed relatives. Upon hearing what had happened, three neighbours who 'had known the child in life and dandled him on their knees' also identified the corpse as being the young Edwin Charles. A muster of police constables was there to ensure that order was maintained, but there is no report of them attempting to stop people taking home the bodies of their dead relatives.

Meanwhile, the police were rather delighted when Howard wrote and informed them that he was travelling from Bakewell to Sheffield on 16 June. His train would reach the Masbrough station in Rotherham and he asked that a police guard meet him to get him safely back to Sheffield. Howard knew there might be a hostile crowd waiting for him, but he had arranged to appear before the magistrates at the Town Hall at twelve o'clock that day in order to pursue his claim for compensation for the destruction of his house. Two Detective Constables, named Airey and Brayshaw, were dispatched to meet the train – though Howard had no idea that they were also carrying a warrant for his arrest. However, when the men arrived at Masbrough station, they found that the train had already arrived and there was no sign of Howard. He must have felt relatively secure in the neighbouring town of Rotherham, as they found him at the Red Lion public house having a drink. He was very surprised when the warrant was produced and he was detained, and it was reported that he appeared nervous and strained, and had difficulty signing documents as his hands were shaking so much. Because of the severity of the charge, which was that he 'had disinterred the bodies of a person or persons unknown', he was advised to employ the services of a solicitor.

Following the disturbances at the cemetery, it had been requested that a proper search for the bodies be undertaken under the surveillance of the Chief Constable the following day. As part of this search the coffin of a child called Gregory, reported missing, was found, but it was deeper in the ground than was expected. Mrs Shearsmith, the mother who had claimed the body of her son, had since made arrangements to have the body reburied and a new nameplate put on the coffin. However, she was now informed that the body of her child had also been found (once again deeper than expected), and she realised with horror that it was a stranger's child she had taken home! As a result of the discovery of coffins where they were supposed to be – i.e. under the ground – Howard's solicitor asked the magistrates to discharge him. The magistrates dismissed the charges regarding the two bodies they had found, but promptly re-arrested him for the removal of the other missing bodies.

At the trial, held the following week, 21 June 1862, the prosecution's story seemed to change. Robert Dixon, in answer to questions from Howard's solicitor, Mr Broadbent, made some replies that cast a different light on his disclosures: he admitted to spending time in prison nine years earlier for stealing barley, and again for shooting hares. Mr Howard suggested that Dixon had fabricated the entire story after he informed the grave-digger that he was no longer welcome to lodge at his house (under suspicion of stealing some of Mr Howard's tools, an accusation denied by Mr Dixon). Dixon was forced to admit that he had been in the house for a full twenty days before he made the hole in the floor, and that although he had shown the coffin nameplates to Mr Oxspring and his colleagues, he had not shown them to the police. The exhibition of the nameplates, it was suggested, had undoubtedly sparked the riot.

In his defence, Howard's solicitor explained that the cemetery was becoming overcrowded, and therefore bodies needed to be dug up and re-buried in the catacombs under the church – on the orders of Revd Livesey, no less. Two other gravediggers, Robert Couldwell and Robert Elliott, also admitted digging bodies out of the graves in the cemetery under Howard's direction. But then came some damning evidence: Micah Hinchcliffe, a chapel keeper of Carver Street, Sheffield, told the court about his son Charles, who had died on 6 May 1858 and was buried on 9 May at St Phillip's. He told the sexton that he wanted his son buried in a select place, as he was 'unable to purchase a headstone at that time'. Howard pointed out a place next to the grave of a woman called Eve Sutcliffe, stating that 'the grave would lie undisturbed for ten years'. Hinchcliffe told the magistrates: 'The child was two years and eleven months when he died. I paid for the grave to be nine feet deep and the coffin had a plate on it which I have identified as coming out of the stable at the cemetery.' He said that that very morning he had searched for his child's grave at the appointed place and had found in its place a large coffin obviously belonging to an adult. The nameplate stated that 'Caroline Wright, died December 20th 1861 aged 34 years' was buried within. The bottom of the grave rested on stone, so he knew that the body of his son could not be beneath the new grave. It had been removed.

Finally Mr Howard was able to speak and defend himself. He stated, rather confusingly, that he had 'been a sexton for thirty years', that he was 'employed as a gravedigger for Revd Livesey since 1857', and that he had 'been a gravedigger ever since'. If Revd Livesey had tried to lay the blame on Howard, then Howard was about to return the favour. He told the jury:

I acted entirely under Revd Livesey's direction and I was paid for the graves I dug and there were no other perquisites. In the latter part of 1861 Livesey gave me permission to disinter bodies that had been interred in 1857-58 and remove them into the catacombs. These were all children. In the register all the bodies that had been removed had a dot put against their names to show that they had been disinterred. A fresh number was given to those who are fresh.

The jury took no time to find him guilty of the charge, and he was sent to the York Assizes for trial.

At the Assizes it was possible that he might have bumped into his old adversary the Revd Livesey, as they were both on trial at the same time! Howard pleaded not guilty to removing dead bodies on 3 June 1862. His defence counsel was Mr Hanney, who made a spirited case for his client. He told the jurors that the offence of disinterring bodies rested on no statute of any Act of Parliament but was rather an offence against the common law of the land (as distinguished from ecclesiastical law). He asked the jury to dismiss from their minds the excitement surrounding the case and anything read in the newspapers so far. The Chief Constable, Mr Jackson, told the jury how he had found a number of empty coffins in the stables which were for the most part in a state of decay. When he entered the catacombs he found eighteen coffins, some standing on end, containing the bodies of young people, aged from a few months to three or four years of age. One coffin was empty. Howard told them that he had emptied the coffins at the direct instructions of Revd Livesey. His defence pointed out that all the work was undertaken during daylight and that Howard did not gain materially by these acts: the sole object was to make room for new bodies. It did not take the jury long to return a verdict of guilty and he was sentenced the next day. The judge, sentencing him to three months' imprisonment, told him that 'his crimes were repugnant to the feelings of mankind even though they were not for any direct gain'. The acts were carried out as a consequence of the overcrowded state of the cemetery, 'but nevertheless it was a practice which should be put a stop to.'

Given the hostility of the locals it is unlikely that Howard returned to Sheffield. People have very long memories, and incidents can sometimes get blown out of all proportion. Howard seems to have been a victim of this. Nevertheless, he could be accused of being sloppy in carrying out his duties – leaving bodies around shows a marked disrespect for the dead of the parish.

At his erstwhile employer's trial, Livesey's solicitor also put up an admirable defence for his client, explaining why the burial service should not have been held over the dissected remains. He again pointed out that the matter was something that should be investigated by the Archbishop of the diocese rather than become a matter of law. He stated that the holding of a burial service was really for the relatives and friends of the deceased who attended the funeral, in order to pay their respects, and therefore such a service should not be held over a box with a dissected body in it. In such cases he felt that the Revd Livesey was correct in assuming that the religious service might be left out. He also felt that the present case and the surrounding publicity was a response to the extravagantly passionate feeling in Sheffield regarding dissection. The actions of the sexton of Hillsborough, Mr Howard, had nothing to do with his client. In his summing up, Livesey's solicitor pointed out that in his naiveté, his client had been misled by the sexton, in good faith, and that he had nothing to gain from omitting a service. Nevertheless, the judge pointed out that Livesey had signed a certificate stating that a service had been held – and that he was therefore guilty of forgery. But his solicitor defended him on this point by saying that he had made the entry on the advice of the sexton, and therefore believed that he was obeying the letter of the law. The jury was out for half an hour and the verdict was 'guilty of making false entries on a death certificate'. The judge, no doubt aware that the matter would go to the diocese, accordingly sentenced him to just three weeks' imprisonment.

The disinterring of bodies by the sexton and the Revd Livesey was quite rightly seen as a disturbing and callous act, disregarding the feelings of the public and of the deceased's relatives. However, when the same act was performed by the police authorities, quietly and by night, it was referred to as an 'exhumation', an event that was necessary in not one but two of the following stories. It is to be hoped that these exhumations were carried out to the letter of the law, and with more respect for the deceased shown by the medical men involved…

Chapter Two

A POISONOUS NURSE?

The Victorian era spawned many crimes of murder by the administration of poison. Such deaths could be hidden from a less-than-diligent surgeon as the unsanitary conditions in which many of the poor people of Sheffield lived frequently resulted in infectious diseases. The following case, however, takes place not in the slums but in a middle-class professional family, who were less at risk from disease, but more at risk, it seems, from their own ill-intentioned staff.

Towards the end of the Victorian period, nursing was becoming a respectable occupation for many women. Nurses were previously notorious for being drunken harridans, shiftless and unclean, but with the emergence of women such as Florence Nightingale nursing began to emerge as the professional occupation it is today. The next case is one where a nurse was charged with poisoning her mistress; she may also have been involved in the mysterious deaths of her mistress's son and daughter. Only towards the end of the trial did another possible suspect emerge. The accounts of the trial include alternate references to strychnine, morphia and opium. Having no background of medicine, I will report it as I have read it and I apologise for any mistakes.

In the summer of 1880 there lived in Sheffield a successful surgeon, Mr W.H. Booth, who had moved to the town from Sharrow about eighteen months previously. He and his family lived in a middle-class suburban area and Mr Booth attended patients at his two surgeries, based at Gell Street and St James Road. He also, on occasion, treated patients from the surgery of his own house, where he kept medicines – including a bottle of strychnine. He lived with his wife, Eliza, and their two children, William Henry Junior and Lucy Ann Jaquette. His life was one of comfort and luxury; then, in 1880, his son was taken ill. As a surgeon he could not treat the boy himself, but he called for the services of a colleague, Mr Pyesmith, to attend him, and he engaged a nurse called Mary Annie Willmott to help with his care. Mr Booth always used the services of nurses from the Sheffield Nurses' Home and apparently was very pleased with the nurses from that establishment. His son's diagnosis proved to be syphilis, and the boy sank rapidly until, on 8 October 1880, he died. Mr Pyesmith wrote out the death certificate, stating the reasons for his death were threefold: he had died from syphilis, paralysis and convulsions.

The whole family was heartbroken. However, before they had time to get over the shock, Lucy Ann Jaquette was also taken ill. At first it was thought that she was suffering solely from the effects of grief, and so Mr Pyesmith was not consulted until two hours before she also died on 16 October. Once again Mr Pyesmith completed the death certificate, stating that she had died from shock arising from grief, convulsions and syncope (fainting). Mrs Booth was understandably devastated at the loss of both her son and daughter, so when she complained of feeling unwell herself on the night that her daughter died she was instructed by Mr Pyesmith to go to bed. She had a friend staying with her to comfort her in her double bereavement, one Harriett W. Harrison; Harriett saw Mrs Booth up to bed and made her comfortable. She also gave Mrs Booth the first dose of the medicine which had been prescribed by Mr Pyesmith.

Mr Pyesmith attended to her on the following day and noted that her hand had started to twitch alarmingly. He prescribed some bromide of potassium and the next day found her a little worse: she was now having convulsions as well as attacks of vomiting. On Tuesday 19 October he consulted with two other doctors, named Thomas and Thorpe, but they could not add any treatment other than that which had been given so far. In the afternoon Willmott, the nurse, appeared in the kitchen and asked the housemaid, Emily Parker, to take the case that she was carrying to Mr Levi Thomas Goucher, the chemist, and ask him to fill up one of the bottles, the one marked opium. (The case in question was small and contained two bottles, one labelled 'opium' and the other 'sal volatile'. Sal volatile was a substance containing ammonia which was used as smelling salts in the Victorian period.) Parker asked if Mrs Booth had asked her to undertake this errand and Willmott told her that she had. In Sheffield there were many chemists and druggists, some better qualified that others. On the evening of Wednesday 20 October, Mrs Booth was given a little drop of whisky and water, but she complained that the mixture was not clear and asked Willmott if the cook had used water from the boiler, which she felt would leave it cloudy. Only taking a small amount, which she later described as a teaspoonful, she refused any more. Half an hour later she had vomited up the remains. On the morning of the next day, 21 October, Mr Pyesmith, who by now was attending her twice a day, found his patient slightly better: he noted that the twitching of her hand had lessened, but he commented that her voice was very slurred and thick. Examining her eyes he found that the pupils were contracted (which indicated the presence of morphine). He asked Willmott if she had given Mrs Booth any morphine, but Willmott denied it. Yet strangely, Willmott once again appeared in the kitchen at 10 a.m. and requested Parker to go to the chemist and take a prescription given to her by Mr Pyesmith. She handed her a piece of paper with writing on which read 'morph.acet.; gras.viii', and she told her that Mr Pyesmith also wanted

Sheffield, showing the rapidly expanding city centre.

a small quantity of charcoal. (Charcoal was often mixed in with morphia in order to distinguish it from other medicines.) When the chemist, Mr Goucher, was asked about this piece of paper in court, he said that the handwriting was that of a medical man with some knowledge of Latin. However, he could not say whose handwriting it was, whether that of Mr Pyesmith or Mr Booth.

The surgeon called again at 6 p.m. the same evening and found Mrs Booth in a coma and insensible, with all the symptoms of 'active and severe narcotic poisoning'. On lifting her eyelids, he found the pupils of her eyes contracted and her face slightly congested. He found that it was impossible to wake her. He asked the nurse how long she had been in that state; she replied, 'since the last cup of tea'. Mr Pyesmith told Willmott that she should have sent for him sooner; she replied that she had sent for him as soon as Mrs Booth appeared faint. He asked for Dr George Thorpe to offer a second opinion. Thorpe felt that her symptoms indicated 'poisoning by opium in some form', and they both agreed that a stomach pump would be the best form of treatment. He called to Mr Booth and asked him to supply him with a stomach pump, which was produced, and injecting some warm water into the pump he flushed the residue from her stomach into another clean basin. He managed to obtain 16ozs of 'coffee-coloured liquid', which he told the nurse he would be sending for analysis. The contents were then poured into a clean container, also produced by Mr Booth.

Thankfully the woman regained consciousness at about 9 p.m. that same evening, although the contraction of her eyes continued for a week after her recovery. Mr Pyesmith had told Willmott quite clearly that if suspicion were to fall on anyone it would be her, as she was the one who had administered all the food and medicine to the patient. His suspicions were indeed aroused, and he told her that he was going to search her room, presumably in order to find out if she had any morphia in her possession. There he found two trunks, one being her own, and one a brown tin trunk which the housemaid had seen her pulling down from the attic lumber-room on the 20th. In the nurse's trunk Mr Pyesmith found little of interest, but when he opened the brown trunk, which had her name on the outside, he found a sealskin coat and other articles belonging to Mrs Booth and the recently deceased Miss Booth. When he asked her how her name had come to be written on the label, she said that the label had probably come unstuck and attached itself to the trunk. He ordered her to return to the Nurses' Home; at first she was reluctant, saying that she had done nothing wrong, but she was eventually persuaded. Another nurse then took her place.

Typical middle-class housing in Gell Street.

Sheffield Nurses' Home, Ecclesfield.

It was agreed that the bodies of the two children should be exhumed during the evening of 1 November 1880 in order to find out more about their sudden deaths; a further post mortem was performed on both. Both bodies were formally identified but the inquest was adjourned until the results of tests on the organs were known. A Sheffield lecturer on toxicology, Mr S. Bell, was present at the post mortem the following day and he supervised the sealing of the organs and the placing of the viscera into clean, carefully labelled jars for transportation to a London hospital where the remains could be analysed. The jars were sealed with string and the surgeon, Mr Arthur Henry Laver, also sealed them with wax on which he placed his initials. Mr Bell then took them to the Medical College Laboratories where they were opened and examined by himself and Dr Tidy, a professor of Chemistry and Forensic Medicine at the London Hospital.

The adjourned inquest on the results of the remains of Master and Miss Booth began on Thursday 2 December 1880 in front of the coroner, Mr D. Wightman. Mr Binney, a solicitor, had been employed to observe the inquest on behalf of Miss Willmott. The coroner invited him to question any of the witnesses if he needed further clarification. Mr Pyesmith was the first to take the stand. He told the inquest about the treatment he had offered for both Master and Miss Booth. The coroner asked him if he had attended the post mortem after the exhumation and he told him that he had. Mr Wightman asked him if he saw anything during the post mortem which would change his mind on his diagnosis of the cause of death for Master Booth, and he stated 'No'. Asked the same question for Miss Booth, however, he replied that he would have changed the primary cause of death from grief to poisoning. He said that after the body of Miss Booth had been exhumed, the limbs of the deceased remained extremely rigid, and the soles of the feet were turned inwards and arched in an unusual manner for a body so long after death. It was well known that spasms attended the bodies of people who had died from strychnine poisoning, but any stiffness of limbs generally disappeared after *rigor mortis* had gone.

Mr Laver, the surgeon, was also present at the post mortem and he told the jury that the body of Master Booth Junior was emaciated and the limbs flaccid. He was asked if he found anything during the post mortem which would prove Mr Pyesmith to be wrong in his diagnosis of the cause of death, and he replied, 'No, sir'. He was asked if there was any appearance of syphilis, but he explained that the brain of the deceased was so destroyed by the first post mortem as to make any examination impossible. He concluded that the second post mortem bore out what was on the certificate: the death was caused by syphilis and convulsions. He was then asked about Miss Booth's remains, which, it seems, were in a good state of preservation for a body which had been buried for a fortnight. He agreed that the lower limbs were still rigid – when he was asked to explain what would cause this condition, he replied that he did not know, and that the rigidity was

Chemist's shop and druggist, *c.* 1930.

'remarkable'. A juror asked him how long rigidity would normally last in a corpse, and he said that typically the rigidity would disappear after twenty-four hours. The coroner asked, 'if poison was administered, would the rigidity last any longer than twenty-four hours?' He replied that 'it did sometimes'.

'Would the administration of strychnine cause such rigidity?' he was asked.

'Maybe, I am not very clear about it,' Mr Laver answered.

The coroner continued, 'Did the body look like a body might look like after getting strychnine poisoning?'

'Yes, it might.'

'Might it look like this without ingesting strychnine poison?'

Again Laver repeated, 'Yes, it might.'

The coroner persisted. 'Suppose death was from natural causes: would you expect rigidity fourteen days after death?'

'I would find it highly improbable.'

The conversation between the two officials does not make the issues any clearer for the layperson or juror to understand: Mr Laver was obviously unable to categorically say what caused the rigidity, or why it persisted so long after death. The questioning continued.

The coroner asked, 'Would any strychnine be in the body fourteen days after death?'

Laver replied, 'It depends how large a dose was administered.'

'Would a small dose be absorbed by the body after death?'

'Yes, it might,' he replied.

The coroner then asked him, 'How much would cause death?'

'About a quarter of a grain.'

One of the jurors, possibly confused by the prevarications, asked whether there were any witnesses who could suggest that any poison had been administered, but the coroner was not willing to undertake this kind of enquiry and reminded them that they should take the word of a medical gentleman. He told them, 'We cannot put ourselves to argue with the testimony of medical gentlemen. Block out any thoughts of poison from your mind.'

But what sealed the decision was the handwritten report from Mr Bell and Dr Tidy, which was produced at the adjourned inquest. The conclusions were unequivocal and read:

> The Laboratory
> London Hospital Medical College
> 28th November 1880
> To Dossey Wightman Esq. Coroner
>
> Re Mr W.H. Booth Junior and Miss L.A.J. Booth
>
> We examined separately several of the organs and viscera for mineral and organic poisons but our results were negative. In our opinion the said W.H. Booth did not die from poison. We examined all the contents of all the bottles for Miss Booth, which were also negative. It is our opinion that Mr Booth and Miss Booth did not die from poison.
>
> Signed Mr Henry S. Bell, Lecturer on Toxicology at Sheffield School of Medicine and Dr C. Memott Tidy, Professor of Chemistry and Forensic Medicine at London Hospital and Medical Officer of Health for Islington.

The jury retired to consider the verdict and when they returned they stated that 'both died without any marks of violence being discovered, but as to the actual cause of death there is not sufficient evidence before the jury to indicate any conclusion'.

The medical investigation of the bodies of the two young people was inconclusive, but it seems that no such ambiguity was left over the illness of Mrs Booth, for the following day Mary Annie Willmott was arrested and charged with administering poison to Mrs Booth with the intention of murdering her. One of the magistrates had ordered her arrest following the inquest, although given the verdict it is difficult to see why. Her solicitor, M. Binney, who had been observing the inquest on behalf of Willmott, went to fetch her to the Town Hall, where she was charged by

Police Constable Thornton. She was taken before the magistrates the following day, but as Mrs Booth was, thankfully, still alive, the surgeon asked that the victim be given a few more days to recover and then her own testimony could be heard. The case was therefore adjourned to Saturday 11 December 1880.

When Miss Willmott came into the court there were many eyes looking in her direction. Although she was only twenty-seven years of age, the reporter noted that she looked much older and 'more haggard' than would have been expected for a woman of her age. He described her as being dressed all in black, even to her black velvet gloves. When it was announced that the first witness would be Mrs Booth, Willmott looked nervously on, but she needn't have worried. Her previous mistress described the events leading up to the deaths of her son and daughter and told the court how happy she had been with the conduct of Miss Willmott throughout. She also stated that it was Miss Willmott who had suggested sending for Drs Thorpe and Thomas when the twitching of her limbs started, which surely would have made her fearful of exposure had she had been guilty of administering the poison. Much was made of the anxiety of the nurse whilst the doctors were attending to Mrs Booth, but this should not necessarily be taken as an outward sign of her guilt.

It seemed that Dr Pyesmith had changed his mind since he last took the stand, for he now told the jury that, on reflection, he thought that Mrs Booth had exhibited signs of strychnine poisoning but it was impossible to be sure. However, he could not explain how it had been administered, as morphine or strychnine given in tea or soup would have alerted the patient due to its bitter and disagreeable taste – though according to a previous statement, the patient had told the doctor that her food tasted 'quite nasty'. The magistrate asked him if her condition could be caused by some kind of nervous shock, but he denied that this would have happened in this particular case. Looking at what she had ingested, Mrs Booth herself had told Dr Pyesmith that her husband had given her some potassium and the prisoner had been in the room when this was discussed. Mrs Booth had asked him not to prescribe opium or morphine as they made her feel ill. He examined her pulse, which was racing, and prescribed digitalis to reduce the heart rate. On the next visit, she told him that she thought there had been some morphia in it as the digitalis had made her ill. He admitted to her that 'it does look as if you have had some'. He asked to see the bottle and it was obvious that only one dose had been used. Significantly, it seems that Mr Booth had made up the medicine from his own surgery. Mr Pyesmith described finding Mrs Booth in an insensible condition. His colleague, Dr George Thorpe, also a surgeon from Sheffield, then took the stand. He concurred with Dr Pyesmith in his diagnosis: when he examined the patient he found her to be lying in bed insensible, her pupils contracted and her breathing very slow. Her symptoms indicated poison by opium in some form or another. The lecturer on toxicology, Mr Bell, then told the court that he had examined the sample retrieved by the stomach pump taken by Mr Pyesmith and had found traces of morphia in it, though he was unable to say in what quantities.

The husband of the victim, Mr Booth, now took the stand. At this point it was noted that the prisoner, who previously had looked tired, began to take a great interest in the proceedings and appeared much calmer than she had before. She seemed to pay great attention to his testimony. The surgeon talked about all three of his surgeries and in particular the contents of the surgery at his home. He said that he kept supplies there, which he would 'top up' when necessary from his own surgeries or from Mr Goucher's shop. In his home surgery he had a desk, and in one of the drawers he had kept a small case with two bottles in. He told the jury that he hadn't used the case for eight or nine years but previously had used them every day for about twenty-five years. The bottles contained a tincture of opium and compound spirit of ammonia. Since Mr Pyesmith commented to him that he felt Mrs Booth had been poisoned, he had searched for the case and the bottles but could find no trace of them. When asked by a juror to describe the last time he had seen the bottles, he stated that he hadn't seen them for between twelve to fourteen weeks. The magistrate asked him if he kept strychnine on the premises at home and he admitted that he did. He described it as a colourless liquid kept in a bottle which he had filled sometime early in October. He also described the day he was called home by the gardener, who told him that his wife's condition was causing some concern; he had returned home immediately. Mr Pyesmith had asked him for a stomach pump and he got one from his surgery. The magistrate asked him who made up the prescriptions ordered for Mrs Booth by Mr Pyesmith and he admitted that he had made them up, but didn't necessarily give them to his wife with his own hands, but 'left them out in the kitchen for someone to take upstairs'. He was questioned about whether he had washed out the bottles before putting in the prescribed medicine and he told the court that he had been meticulous, as would any doctor. When asked about his wife vomiting after the whisky and water, he claimed that his wife was 'sick most days'.

Mr Booth's demeanour on the stand was quite noticeably different when being questioned about the strychnine: the reporter stated that he appeared in 'a very excitable manner', though previously he had given his evidence in a very controlled way. Was it Mr Pyesmith's impression that Mrs Booth had been poisoned that had rattled him? When asked if his attention had been brought to the strychnine in October, his composure seems to have broken – 'Alas, yes, it was,' he replied, and gave way to 'great emotion'. Incredibly, at that point in the trial he looked across to the prisoner and made a deprecatory motion with his hand at her, at the same time shaking his head. In reply she smiled at him. The defence declared that he had shaken his fist at her (although if he had, it would have been difficult to see why she smiled).

The inquiry continued – as did Mr Booth's bizarre behaviour. It was reported that he moved about in the witness box as if he couldn't stand still, and his statements were delivered in a fast staccato fashion. He was told several times by the magistrates to calm himself and he replied, 'Oh, if you knew as much as I do,' and he burst into tears, saying, 'it cuts me, it cuts me.' Once again he was urged to calm down and a chair was found for him. He again repeated that the bottle of strychnine had been filled up from his other surgery as his home supply had been depleted. When asked why his stock had disappeared, he said that it was from 'having to prescribe it for many patients'. When asked to name any of the patients, however, he was not able to think of a single name. He estimated that the bottle had been in the house for at least eighteen months. He told the court that strychnine was often used in medicine, 'as any doctor will tell you', and he pointed out that Dr Branson had prescribed it for his daughter about a year previously.

Mr Pyesmith's housekeeper, Martha Barwick, then took the stand and recalled that she had gone to the Booths' house with a message for the doctor on Sunday 17 October 1880. Whilst waiting for him in the kitchen – and near to the passage leading to Dr Booth's surgery – she saw the nurse in the passageway with a bottle of colourless liquid and a measuring spoon. She appeared to be measuring some liquid into the spoon, but realising that she had put too much in she returned it back to the bottle and measured it out once more. Martha maintained that the bottle contained strychnine and had come from Dr Booth's surgery. However, when questioned she told the jury that there had been some writing on the bottle, but she was too far away to see what was written on it.

Finally Miss Willmott took the stand. The court was silent, and it was reported that 'one could hear a pin drop'; the local interest in the case was intense. She told the court that it had been her suggestion to call in the doctors as Mrs Booth's condition worsened. She had asked the housemaid Parker to call Dr Thorpe, but Parker told her that Mrs Booth didn't like Dr Thorpe. In the end Mr Pyesmith was sent for. She talked about the occasion when she had brought the tin trunk into her room, for the purpose, she said, of storing some of Miss Booth's clothing; that she had no intention of stealing the clothes, although she could not explain why a label with her name on had been found on the trunk. Willmott pointed out that although she had given both medicine and food to Mrs Booth, both items had been prepared by the cook or Mr Booth himself. (One of the most curious points of this mysterious case was that the cook, Mrs Florence Horton, had left the country following Mrs Booth's illness. However, I could not find any mention of whether the disappearance of this witness had been followed up. I would have thought that this would have been a very important witness, particularly as she had prepared all the food given to Mrs Booth, a point which the prisoner brought to the attention of the court.) Willmott stated that:

I would like to say sir that I am innocent of the charges made against me. I never sent Emily Parker to Mr Goucher's for morphia or anything else that would be likely to injure Mrs Booth and that I only gave her food and medicine, which had already been prepared for me. I should have been sorry to injure any of Mrs Booth's family. They were all very kind to me. That is all I wish to say.

No further witnesses were called for the defence.

The judge summed up: it was an incontrovertible fact, he said, that traces of poison had been found in the stomach of Mrs Booth. The points that the jury had to consider were threefold: whether poison had been given to Mrs Booth, and if so who had administered it and with what intention. Mr Seymour, for the defence, stated that he could not name any motive for Willmott to have committed the crime: that there was no evidence of any feelings of revenge or any great hope of benefit from the crime for her. There was nothing but a 'miserable box and its trumpery contents'. Willmott made no attempt to hide the stolen items, and there was no evidence that she had taken anything else from Mrs or Miss Booth. The jury retired to discuss the case and was gone for two hours and forty minutes. When they returned to the court at 8.45 p.m. they gave their verdict: they found that the prisoner had administered morphia to Mrs Booth, but with what intention they could not determine. The judge replied, 'You found that she had administered poison but without intent to murder her mistress?' The foreman replied, 'Yes, my lord'. The judge informed him that that amounted to a 'not guilty verdict', and the prisoner was discharged.

This case was a curious one, to say the very least. Mr Booth's reaction to the questions about the strychnine was puzzling and bizarre. This was a professional man, who would no doubt in the course of his work regularly have to give evidence in court. I would also suggest that perhaps his relationship with the nurse might have needed more scrutiny, but it is impossible to tell from this distance in time. Doctors and surgeons of the Victorian period were often afforded an almost god-like status, and would therefore not have been questioned by a magistrate. The words to the jury that they 'could not put their minds against the testimony of medical men' spoke all too clearly of the esteem in which doctors were held. Fellow doctors might also take a stand against any information that would bring their position into disrepute. In the middle of all this was a nurse who was vilified from the start of the case – and therefore her discharge was all the more puzzling. Morphia was used as a form of pain relief in the Victorian period and it could be that, to ease Mrs Booth's distress, she gave her some and then denied it, but would she have done this knowing that Mrs Booth suffered an allergic reaction to opium or morphia? It is hardly likely. My belief is that the professional people concerned in this case were all too aware of the real villain of the piece, but their identity is something that we will never know.

Chapter Three

THE CURIOUS TALE OF MRS GLOSSOP

Whilst researching another case I came across the curious tale of Mrs Glossop, a case where, once again, the body of a suspected victim of poisoning was exhumed two weeks after she died. What fascinated me as a researcher was the startlingly modern lifestyle of the victim. Mrs Hannah Eliza Glossop was a free spirit who flouted Victorian attitudes towards respectability to be with the man that she loved. The gossip about her lifestyle was no doubt the reason behind an anonymous letter which was sent to the Chief Constable asking him to investigate her death. Her demise appeared, on the surface, to be a tragic death caused by puerperal fever in a young woman following the miscarriage of a four-month-old foetus. But, as revelations at the inquest would show, the case was far from normal. The dangers of giving birth in the Victorian period often led to the death of both mother and child. If the poor medical skill of the midwives didn't get you, the fevers brought on by lack of hygiene and lack of skills probably would. Victorian doctors had very few reliable medicines to treat post-natal symptoms, and they would often prescribe alcohol instead, which in those days was believed to be a stimulant back to health.

Mrs Glossop lived with her mother at the house at 17 Howard Street. Her mother took in lodgers, and one of those lodgers was George Davies, who preferred to use the name 'Dr Henry'. Mrs Glossop was a married woman who had suffered a second miscarriage the previous year, in August 1852, whilst her husband Charles and her brother were on the point of sailing to Australia to search for gold. (Gold had recently been found in Australia and thousands of English prospectors were flooding to the country to seek their fortune.) With her husband out of the way, it seems that the path was clear for Mrs Glossop to step out with Dr Henry – and step out they did. Flouting convention, they were often seen out in public together, and even went on holiday together (with the full blessing of Hannah's mother, who readily admitted to the scandalised magistrate and jury to helping her daughter get ready to go out with her admirer). The mother was also seen in a carriage with her daughter, Dr Henry and her grandchild on outings in and around the Sheffield area. Naturally the rumour-mongers of the town disapproved of this sort of behaviour, and it wasn't long before tittle-tattle was heard to say that Mr Glossop had left because of Mrs Glossop's behaviour with Dr Henry (who had lodged at the house for over two years).

More gossip flew after the curious death of Mrs Glossop – had her lover Dr Henry poisoned her? It seems that she had not been in the best of health since the miscarriage the previous August, and that before her death Dr M.M. Bartelome had been called in, on Monday 2 May 1853, to attend her. The doctor was not informed about the miscarriage; he was just told that she had developed a fever. Dr Bartelome also called in another surgeon, Dr Barber, for a second opinion, and they concluded that she was suffering from a fever of the brain. The poor girl declined very quickly in health and when the doctors visited on 9 May they found her in a semi-conscious state. The pupils of her eyes were dilated and she never spoke or moved again. Dr Bartelome recommended that a blister be placed on the back of the neck. This old remedy was usually a mustard blister, which would cause blisters to form on the skin. The doctor would drain these, and it was believed that the infection would be drained from the body at the same time. In truth, he recognised that the poor woman was too far gone to save, but he did what he could to help her. A hairdresser from Norfolk Street, a Mr Henry Norton, was called in to cut off her hair and shave her head prior to the blister being applied. Mr Norton told the coroner and the jury at the inquest that whilst he was in Mrs Glossop's bedroom attending to her, the mysterious Dr Henry came in and gave Mrs Glossop a dose of white mixture from a bottle that a servant had brought into the room. The mother of Mrs Glossop, Mrs Simpson, also came in and gave her daughter either a small brandy or a mixture of wine and water – he couldn't be sure. The doctor asked her what had afflicted her daughter and Mrs Simpson said it was 'the purging'. In the Victorian era there were various remedies for purging after birth, which was thought to rid the woman's body of all those ill-humours caused during pregnancy.

The poor girl died shortly afterwards, and a Mrs Ann Camm of 21 Eyre Street was called in to lay out the body. Although she admitted that she did not know Mrs Glossop previously, she was quick to spread the gossip about her. It seems that as she left the deceased's house, she told the police that she spoke to a man who she thought was 'Mr Clubb, who was Dr Gregory's man'. In reply to a question about where she had been engaged, he asked her if that was the house where Dr Henry lived. She acknowledged that it was, and he mysteriously stated that 'she will have been poisoned then'. This curious statement was told to the coroner, who naturally wanted to question her more clearly about the mysterious man. Despite having said his name was 'Mr Clubb', Mrs Camm now denied that she knew him. The coroner tried to get her to find out the name of this stranger, but she said that the rumours had it that Mrs Glossop had been poisoned an hour after she had died, and that all Eyre Street knew about it.

Above left: No. 17 Howard Street.

Above right: Dr Bartelome.

Left: Norfolk Street in 1890.

The gossipmongers did their work so well that shortly afterwards a letter was sent to the Chief Constable (who at the time was a Mr Raynor) stating these rumours as fact and calling for an investigation into the curious death of this twenty-six-year-old woman. The Chief Constable made some enquiries of the doctors who had treated her. They both said that she had died from fever and effusions of blood on the brain. One of her carers, Mary Hattersley of Bramall Lane, told Mr Raynor that she had been with Mrs Glossop just before she died, and that she had given her some wine and brandy which had been ordered for her by Dr Barber. She had only taken a little, but she had been pretty insensible during the following night. The Chief Constable felt that there was enough evidence to look more closely into the circumstances of the woman's death and ordered that the body be exhumed during the night of 23/24 May 1853 from St George's churchyard. Seven medical gentlemen, including Drs Barber and Bartelome, carried out the post mortem on the exhumed corpse. They found that the deceased had died from fever, which had been brought on by her miscarriage of a four-month-old foetus. Dr Henry was summoned to the Town Hall and was questioned about his involvement with Mrs Glossop, as a result of which he was placed in custody until the inquest at the Beehive Inn, Glossop Road the following day. As was usual, the jury inspected the gruesome remains, held in one of the entrance porches of St George's Church.

At the start of the inquest it seems that Dr Henry had not arrived; however, the coroner was informed that he was on his way escorted by two police constables. The coroner opened the inquest by questioning the deceased woman's mother, Mrs Simpson. She stated that she was a widow of the late William Simpson, a dye-maker of Sheffield. She was then asked a series of questions that almost became a comedy routine, as the coroner desperately tried to maintain his dignity. He began by asking her about her daughter's relationship with Dr Henry, whom she called 'an innocent young man, sir'. He reproved her for this statement, saying that it was inappropriate that she make such remarks and pointing out that it was the jury's responsibility to prove innocence. Suitably admonished, he asked her if her daughter and Dr Henry 'often stayed out late, for example until one o'clock in the morning.'

'No sir, we are always in bed by twelve, sir.'

'Did your daughter and Dr Henry go to the theatre together?' he asked.

'Sometimes, but they were always in early.'

'Did your daughter and Dr Henry go out in a carriage together?'

She replied, 'Yes, and he frequently took her out, her and the child in the gig and I came too.'

Eyre Street in 1910.

Above left and right: Bramall Lane and Cherry Street in 1910, and a postcard showing the vicars of St George's Church and the church itself in 1876.

'Had there been any problems in the marriage of Mr and Mrs Glossop?'

'No sir, it was a love match.'

He continued to question her, asking, 'Did Mr Glossop ever express any jealousy towards Dr Henry?'

'No, he idolised her. Never was there a more affectionate couple.'

'Did Dr Henry give your daughter anything?'

'I don't know that he gave her any medicine of any kind.'

Getting to the crux of the matter, he asked her, point blank, 'Had you noticed any intimacy between your daughter and Dr Henry?'

'No sir, nothing more than would have been if her husband had been at home.'

Mrs Simpson told the coroner that her daughter had had a miscarriage just before her husband went to Australia the previous August and that she had never been well since. She told the inquest about calling in Dr Barber to see her daughter on Monday 2 May 1853, and how despite his attentions she died on Tuesday 10 May and was interred in St George's churchyard the following Friday, 'in the same grave as her papa'. The coroner asked her: 'Has your daughter had a miscarriage since the one in August of last year?'

At this point Mrs Simpson, disregarding the medical evidence to the contrary, lied. She told him, 'No sir, she has not. She was four months gone when she miscarried in August', a tragedy she attributed to the fact that she had 'worked so hard packing for her husband and her brother'.

Then Dr Henry arrived at the inquest. As well as the constables he was attended by two solicitors, Mr Fretson and Mr Ferrall, both of whom were introduced to the coroner as his 'advisors'. They asked the permission of the coroner to take notes and to ask the witnesses some questions, and the coroner agreed that they could. The coroner then explained that the jury had been summoned to look into the death of Hannah Eliza, the wife of Charles Glossop. He then asked Dr Henry to state his name. Mr Fretson answered on behalf of the witness, stating that 'his real name is George Davies but his professional name is Dr Henry as he is part of the firm of Henry and Co.' It seems that Dr Henry was in partnership with his brother Joseph in Sheffield and his other brother Charles in Manchester. Through his advisors he was asked what his professional role was, and he told the inquest that he was a 'patent medicine proprietor'. The coroner asked who he was in partnership with at the present and he stated that he was on his own at the moment. The coroner asked him to clarify his status, and asked, 'are you a medical practitioner?' He replied that he wasn't.

'Were you at any medical college?'

'No, sir.'

'Do you practice surgery?'

'No sir,' he replied.

He told the coroner that he was only licensed to sell patent medicine. The coroner explained the reasons for the enquiries: 'I only put these questions to you as you advertise under the name of Dr Henry of Henry and Co.'

'That was because it was a family name,' he replied, 'and the company carried on the profession in Manchester for fourteen to fifteen years.'

Mr Fretson, possibly in order to divert the coroner from the question of the professional status of the doctor, told him that 'the stories regarding the mysterious death of Mrs Glossop have been discussed in public and Dr Henry is exceedingly anxious that the matter should be cleared up'.

The coroner then discussed the gossip surrounding the funeral of the deceased. He asked Dr Henry: 'Were there some irregularities at the interment where people in charge of the funeral were tipsy?' Mrs Simpson interrupted at this point saying, 'Yes, but alcohol wasn't given to them – they took it.' With some patience the coroner reiterated: 'There was great drunkenness at the funeral. One of the pallbearers was ill used and one was sent to the Town Hall and there was fighting. Didn't some of the parties act disgracefully?' Without giving Dr Henry the chance to reply, Mrs Simpson said, 'They did, sir.' '

As a result of this, a communication was sent to Mr Raynor implying that Mrs Glossop's death was due to Dr Henry?' Once more she intervened before Dr Henry could reply: 'Nothing of the kind sir.'

By now the coroner had had enough and snapped at her: 'You had better withdraw madam or not interrupt me.' Still she insisted on having the last word, stating 'Excuse me sir, but it is false.' At this point Mrs Simpson asked if she could join Dr Henry on the bench and the coroner, no doubt to shut her up, agreed. She walked over to where he sat and in an exaggerated manner placed both arms on his shoulders and kissed him. Ignoring this display of affection, the coroner continued questioning Dr Henry. He suggested that the deceased had conducted herself 'with some levity', and it had been rumoured that her husband had separated from her and gone to Australia because of her conduct. Dr Henry told him that he had lodged with the family for some time, but there had been no dispute with her husband. The coroner then informed the jury that 'as a consequence of the communication an allegation was made that something had been given to the deceased and an exhumation was ordered on the body of Mrs Glossop.'

Mr Fretson then asked the inquest if he might ask Mrs Simpson some questions and the coroner agreed. She was reminded that she was still on oath and he asked her, 'Did your daughter complain of any improper treatment from anyone?'

'Oh no sir, we all idolised her,' she replied.

'When she went out with Dr Henry was it with your permission?' he enquired.

'Always sir, I was glad for him to take her out and I have been with them many a time too. I have fixed her bonnet, and got her ready to go out with him many times.'

Mr James F. Wright, who had undertaken the post mortem, now took the stand. He stated that at the post mortem he had been witnessed by six other doctors, who were Messrs Bartelome, Mr William Jackson, Mr Lewis, Mr Barber, Mr G. Atkins and Mr Herbert Walker. He stated that the cause of death was a coma arising from an intense congestion of the brain and effusions of blood in its substance. He offered his opinion that the womb had previously held a foetus that had been expelled four months after conception. All the medical men concurred with him on the cause of death. He was asked by the coroner if he thought that the foetus had been expelled by force and Mr Wright replied that he didn't think so.

'Was an instrument used, could you say?' the coroner asked.

'There was a slight abrasion to the uterus but not withstanding that, I cannot say if force had been used,' he replied.

'Was it yours or any other medical person's opinion that the foetus was expelled recently or as long ago as August of last year?' the coroner asked him. 'Much more recently,' he replied. 'It was our opinion that it had happened about three to four weeks previously. The contents of the stomach were to be analysed for any sign of poison and her breast still expelled small amounts of milk.'

Dr Bartelome next gave evidence. He stated that he had been called to see Mrs Glossop at 9 a.m. on the morning of 9 May. She was lying on her back unable to move. Her heart was beating rapidly and she was very weak. He said that his patient was labouring under considerable irritation of the brain. Mr Barber was unable to attend the inquest as it was reported to the coroner and the members of the jury that he was on duty with the Yeomanry Cavalry at Doncaster. Upon hearing about the inquest he had returned to Sheffield and had consulted with Dr Bartelome but had since been forced to return to Doncaster. It was agreed that the inquest would be adjourned to the following Tuesday at 6 p.m. to await the analysis of the stomach contents, and in the hope that Dr Barber would be able to attend.

The following week, the adjourned inquest continued. It is interesting to note that in the *Sheffield and Rotherham Independent*'s version of events Dr Henry is no longer given the title of 'doctor': throughout the report he is referred to as 'Mr Davies'. A servant of Mrs Simpson was the first to give evidence, which once again focused on the intimate relationship between Mrs Glossop and Mr Davies. She said that she had been employed by Mrs Simpson for five years, but had left her establishment five months previously. She told the coroner that since Mr Glossop had gone to Australia she had often seen familiarities between Mrs Glossop and Mr Davies and she had witnessed the deceased sitting on his knee. She had seen her lay her arm on his shoulders and kiss him. She also reported an occasion when Mrs Glossop had been in his bedroom during the afternoon with the door locked. She had been told to make the bed afterwards and it bore the imprint of two people on it. In reply to a question from the coroner, she said that she had never seen Mr Davies give Mrs Glossop any medicine. Once more going back to the time when the couple returned home from outings, one of the jury asked if they had stayed out longer than 11 p.m. She replied that she had known them stay out longer than 11 p.m., but apart from when they had holidayed together she had not known them to stay out all night.

Dr Bartelome took the stand and told the inquest that he had certified death as being from 'fever and effusions of blood on the brain'. He told the court that, given the statements from Mrs Simpson and Mrs Glossop at the time he was called in to attend to her, and the fact that the subject of a miscarriage had not been mentioned to him, he had examined her only for a brain fever. Now being fully aware of the facts he felt that the death of Mrs Glossop was probably from puerperal fever. He was unable to be more certain as he had not physically examined Mrs Glossop to establish whether she had given birth. Dr James Haywood, a professional chemist, stated that having analysed the stomach contents, he could not find the slightest trace of a vegetable or mineral poison.

Then the inquest took a strange turn which indicated that some enquiries had been made into the background of Mr Davies. The coroner asked him if he had ever lived in York and he replied that he had.

'Have you lived in Gillygate in York?' the coroner questioned.

'Yes,' Davies replied.

'For how long?'

'I cannot speak of any time.'

'You cannot say whether you lived there for six weeks or six months?' the coroner incredulously enquired.

Curiously, Davies retorted, 'I must decline answering such a question.'

The coroner then asked him why he had left York, but Davies declined to answer once again. His advisor, Mr Fretson, no doubt trying to change the tone of the inquiry, informed the coroner that he wished to tell the inquest why Davies left Sheffield on the morning before Mrs Glossop died. The coroner refused to listen to the explanations, and stated that unless Mr Davies would like to give the explanation himself he was not prepared to listen. After a short consultation with Mr Fretson, Davies told him that he had left Sheffield on the Tuesday as a result of what Dr Barber had said to him. The contents of this conversation are not known, as Davies once again declined to specify. After hearing all the evidence, the jury retired to discuss the verdict. When they returned, they told the coroner that in their opinion Mrs Glossop had died from a coma arising from inflammation of the brain as a consequence of having recently been delivered of a foetus, but 'whether it was induced naturally or unnaturally there is not sufficient evidence to prove'. If the medical men were correct in their estimate of the date of the miscarriage (and of course, the possibility remains that Hannah had not miscarried as she had thought before her husband left, but lost the baby a short while later), the baby, the loss of which caused the death of young Hannah, seems likely to have been Dr Henry's, but whether he had anything to do with the miscarriage that followed must remain unsolved. Mr Booth, the foreman of the jury, added that the 'jury beg to express their strong opinion as to the propriety and levity of the conduct not only of Mrs Simpson and her late daughter but of Mr Davies himself'. Mr Davies was then discharged.

It would seem likely that both Mrs Simpson and Mrs Glossop wanted to share in the respectability attached to doctors. To be reduced to 'a seller of quack medicine' would have humiliated Davies at the inquest. So it is not without irony that No. 17 Howard Street was later the home of W. Wilkinson and Co., listed as Patent Medicine Vendors, a position which was less esteemed towards the end of the Victorian period. In this case it was not the position he held, or the circumstances surrounding the death of Mrs Glossop, but the behaviour of all the suspects which condemned them. From our modern perspective, we might admire Mrs Glossop for taking the stance that she did, but it was considered to be unacceptable by her Victorian counterparts. The concentration on the time that the couple came home from outings is mysterious to our modern ears, and again seemed to be considered not quite respectable. But there is no doubt that, whatever the behaviour of the parties concerned, the circumstances created led to the death of a young woman in the prime of her life, and that gossip fuelled the case that was built around her paramour.

Chapter Four

DEATH AT THE MAIL COACH INN

The Victorian period saw the emergence of Temperance Leagues, where upright citizens of the town would sign a pledge to never drink alcohol. Sheffield had more than its fair share of pubs, inns and beerhouses and the many attempts to limit drinking hours were never very successful in the town. New beerhouses could spring up overnight. No one could predict when drink-fuelled violence was going to occur, and so when Aaron Allinson decided on an impulse to have one drink before turning in for the night, he had no idea that he had but minutes to live. He was walking with his daughter, Mrs Ross, past the Mail Coach Inn on West Street, Sheffield at 11.20 p.m. on the night of Saturday 26 August 1865, when he decided that he was going to have a last pint of beer. Mrs Ross urged him, 'Don't be long, father.' Allinson promised his daughter that he would return home to 7 Broomhall Lane for some supper very soon. Allinson was aged fifty-six and was a widower who had lived with his daughter since the death of his wife. He was described as a well-respected man, well-liked and cheerful, but was also something of an innocent (or what we would call today 'not very streetwise').

As he went into the public house, which was at that time of night quite crowded, he took his glass of beer and went to talk to some friends. What happened next was the subject of much debate (both in and out of the courtroom). It seems that a party of about five or six men had come into a room known as 'the vault' just before Allinson arrived – and they were definitely out to cause trouble. Two of them in particular, both Irishmen, were notorious in the area: Peter Devine (aged twenty-four) and James Doyle (twenty-five). Both men had a record of violence, and had been involved in the shooting of Police Constable Smith two months earlier on 25 June 1865. The case against the pair had been dismissed because there was not enough evidence to convict them (although two other acquaintances, Coffey and Hannigan, had also been sent to trial for the crime). Both Devine and Doyle were residents of Charlotte Street, and both were well known to the police for their part in previous pub brawls.

They certainly seemed determined to pick a fight that evening, and they did not seem to care with whom. Devine first tried to pick a fight with Henry Thomas Thompson, an employee at the Mail Coach Inn; although the latter told Devine that he had no

An unnamed beerhouse in Church Street, 1870.

The Mail Coach Inn, West Street.

quarrel with him, Devine struck him. His father, Thomas Kay Thompson, who also worked at the pub, shouted, 'Don't be a fool – for God's sake, let us not have a fight at this time of night.' There were only forty minutes left until closing time. Devine then attacked the elder Thompson for calling him 'a fool'. At this point in the affray, and no doubt in an attempt to pacify the situation, Allinson stood up and said, 'let us have no rowing.' Doyle then struck Allinson, who fell to the floor. The two men started to kick the old man in the legs and arms. Witnesses agreed that Allinson had not struck either of the men or provoked them in any way. Thompson could not believe this was happening at this late hour; the party of men had only been in the pub for twenty minutes. It was reported that Allinson was sober and was generally an easy-going man who got on well with people. The fight was over in about three minutes.

Thompson saw that the poor man was in a very serious condition. John Warren, a shoemaker of Edward Street who also worked in the Mail Coach Inn, said that Henry Thompson had previously been chaffing with Devine, although he could not hear what the men were talking about, and he was surprised when Devine had followed him into a corner and struck at him. Realising that a fight was breaking out, Thompson had leapt over the counter to open a 'little door' to let the other customers out. When he next saw the fighting, he saw Allinson on the floor with the two men kicking him.

One of the courts off Charlotte Street.

Edward Street.

The landlord of the Mail Coach Inn saw very little of the start of it. He had been serving customers in the other bar until he heard the sounds of a fight in the vault and went in to see what was happening – then he also was attacked by Doyle. He stated categorically that the public house had been quiet and orderly before the prisoners came in. Mrs Ross was sent for. She arrived to find her father stretched out insensible on a piece of furniture known as a longsettle. Mr Robert Hewer, the surgeon of St George's Square, was called in to attend to the elderly man a little before midnight, and he quickly realised that it was too late: Allinson was already dead. Thompson, seeing the state of the body, ordered his colleagues to lock the door of the public house in the hope of keeping the miscreants inside the pub until the police arrived. But by this time, Doyle had gone. When Thompson next saw him he was at the Town Hall and he had changed his clothes.

Another witness, John Alsopp of Broomhall Street, saw the old man being knocked down, and he reported that he fell on his right side. However, he was unable to say whether his head struck the floor. All the witnesses agreed that the attack was a wanton and unprovoked assault on a man who was just trying to calm the situation.

On Monday 28 August, the inquest was heard at the Sheffield Dispensary before the coroner, Mr J. Webster Esq. The prisoners were brought into the room and were described by the reporter as being 'both young but not very intelligent in appearance'. Mr Robert Hewer, the surgeon, was the first to take the stand. He told them that he had attended the deceased at the public house and had undertaken the post mortem. He found a small lacerated wound on the left side of the nose about an inch long; there were several contusions on the head and upper part of the body, contusions on the right arm from the shoulder to the elbow, others on the right thigh and five abrasions on the left leg. On lifting the skull he found blood on the brain and noted that it was very congested. The chest and lungs were healthy but the heart was rather large and flabby. This, he assured the coroner, would not have caused the man's death: indeed, there was no injury in any other part of the body which could have caused his death. He told the jury that the cause of death was the effusion of blood on the brain caused by a blow or a fall. A heavy blow on the head with a fist or a kick would have done it. The coroner asked him if death could have been caused by his head hitting the floor of the vault (which was made of stone) and the surgeon agreed that it might have contributed to Allinson's death.

Thomas Thompson, who had worked at the pub, appeared before the inquest with a bruised face and an enormous black eye, sustained in the fight. He was not allowed to give his account of the fight as Doyle kept interrupting his evidence. Thompson told the jury that the men had come in looking for a fight, but Doyle shouted across the room at him, 'Where are the other men in the house that instigated the row?' Thompson told him that there were no other instigators of the fight.

St George's Square.

Sheffield
Public
Hospital and
Dispensary.

'Were there not ten or twelve men in the house that night?'

'There might have been,' Thompson answered.

'Did you see me strike the old man?' he demanded.

'Yes,' he replied.

'It was only once,' Doyle said.

'Yes, but you repeatedly kicked him while he was on the floor.'

It seems that Doyle was hoping to undermine the credibility of the witness, as he then called out, 'Did you see me leave?'

'No,' Thompson replied.

'You would have seen me leave if you had been sober.'

The coroner asked Thompson if he saw the deceased strike either of the prisoners, and he told him that he hadn't. One of the jurors asked, 'Were any words spoken between the prisoners and the deceased?' Thompson told them that no words had passed between them. The same juror stated that there must have been some kind of provocation, but the coroner interjected, stating that 'it is not at all necessary for a jury to prove that there should be any provocation'. The coroner told the inquest that there were other witness statements about the incident, but there seemed to be little point in calling for any more: the jury had heard from the evidence of five or six witnesses that the deceased was kicked and struck by the prisoners whilst lying on the floor. He instructed the jury to consider whether there was any provocation or any justification for the attack, or if it was done through sheer wantonness. They had to decide whether it was murder or manslaughter. He added: 'There was nothing in my opinion to justify this attack. The prisoners were guilty of violence which was intended to do grievous bodily harm, and as death had resulted then it was murder. If the jury finds any provocation then it would be manslaughter.'

Following this statement, there was a short deliberation in private before a verdict of wilful murder was given against Doyle and Devine. The two men were called back into the room to hear the verdict and the coroner made out the warrant for their committal to Leeds Assizes. They were then removed to the cells at the Town Hall.

The two prisoners were put on trial at Leeds in front of Mr Justice Shee on Monday 16 January 1866. But before the trial started, his Lordship stated that he had an announcement to make: he told the court that the evidence of Henry Thompson could not be heard as he had an affliction of the brain and was for the present an inmate of a lunatic asylum! Furthermore, the witness John Warren could not give his evidence as he was suffering from a disease of the lung. It was highly unusual that two witnesses to a crime could not attend for medical reasons, and so the judge demanded to see medical reports confirming their illness, which were produced. It was agreed that the trial would continue without the evidence of these two men.

Surgeon Mr Robert Hewer then took the stand, and his testimony as to the cause of death was somewhat altered: he stated that the cause of death was a blow, a kick or a fall. As there were slate tiles on the floor of the vault, he now gave his opinion that death probably resulted when the deceased's head came into contact with a hard surface. He pointed out that although many people had witnessed the attack and the prisoners kicking the man once he was on the floor, not one had reported them kicking him in the head. It was therefore his opinion that the deceased fell and from that fall he died. (Previously, of course, he thought the fall only a possible contributing factor.) This surprising opinion, combined with the sudden non-appearance of two key witnesses, does suggest that witness intimidation might have been employed, though that of course is only an opinion.

The judge concluded by addressing the jury, stating that there was no doubt in his mind that Aaron Allinson met his death through violence committed by the prisoners. There was also no doubt that the men were in a state of extreme excitement and were determined to pick a fight. The deed was not done in the heat of passion, nor did they have a quarrel with the deceased, and therefore he recommended the jury to return a verdict of manslaughter. The jury retired and within a few minutes came back with a verdict according to the judge's recommendation. Before being removed from the dock, Doyle shouted out that he had never seen the deceased in his life, although being tried with Devine, he knew who did the harm. The judge sentenced the prisoners to fifteen months' hard labour, and added that in his opinion the jury came to the right verdict.

No doubt the police force in Sheffield were glad to have a respite from the criminal activities of this pair, but sadly vicious acts like these were a common occurrence in the area for many years to come. However, not all crimes were carried out in the public arena: many occurred in quiet and domestic spaces in ordinary households...

Chapter Five

CRIMES OF BIGAMY

There are many reasons why people commit bigamy, but mostly the reasons are selfish and opportune. It was no different in the Victorian period. But the moral code which ruled Victorian society was not applied in the same way across the social spectrum: bigamy appears to have been viewed as almost acceptable amongst working-class Victorians. It was tolerated so long as there was a genuine reason for the first marriage to have ended: a partner's alcoholism, say, or mental health issues which would force one partner to abandon another. It has even been said that this crime was 'a poor man's divorce'. Victorian novels often used bigamy as a favourite theme, such as in *Jane Eyre* by Charlotte Bronte, *Man and Wife* by Wilkie Collins and *Lady Audley's Secret* by Mary Elizabeth Braddon. Middle or upper-class people, of course, viewed this crime differently, as it raised issues of inheritance and social status. The following case began with a young woman who felt oppressed by her father, and preferred the blandishments of a young man to the prospect of remaining in her home. She abandoned her family home on 2 October 1880.

Charles Butler, a confectioner of Snig Hill, Sheffield, had employed Henry Samuel George Burton (aged twenty-three) in 1877. Married with two young children, Burton's career as a baker came to an end when he was convicted of robbing Mr Butler and was sentenced to three months' imprisonment. Whilst he was serving this prison sentence, Mr Butler opened another eating-house in Snig Hill, an establishment which was run by his daughter Annie Elizabeth. Mr Butler was therefore surprised when he received a letter from Burton on 31 July 1880 asking for a meeting. Burton travelled up from Normanton on the appointed day and had a sad tale to tell his previous employer: he told him that he was in terrible trouble, and that, after leaving prison, his wife Mary and both of his children had died. He asked Butler if he would employ him again, and promised him that things would be different this time as he had 'turned over a new leaf'. Butler agreed. Sadly for him, in doing so he had taken a snake to his bosom.

Burton started work at the eating-house and became friendly with Miss Butler. He told her the story of the last few weeks of his family's lives: how his wife had

Snig Hill, 1890.

been so ill that only he and the nurse were allowed in the sick room; how he had been devoted to his wife, who had been so weak that he was forced to carry her from place to place. However, when he told her that turf had been put on the road outside to deaden the sound of passing traffic, she began to question the truthfulness of his story. Despite this, he touched her heart when he told her about the funeral of his wife and children, and how he had been mad with grief for three weeks after her death. Talking to Miss Butler obviously cheered him, as it was not long before he started to pay court to her. Before long he asked her to marry him. She at first refused, but finally, on Friday 1 October, she agreed. He told her that he did not want her father to know about it as he would try to talk her out of it – and as relations between Miss Butler and her father were very strained, she agreed.

They made plans to marry at a church in Sheffield as soon as possible. In order to keep the plans secret, the pair agreed that she would leave home and go into lodgings until the day of their wedding. He found her some lodgings at the house of Mr Mirfin on Alderson Road. The very next day, after she had closed the eating house at 11 p.m., Miss Butler abandoned her father's house in Fargate and went to her new home. Mr Butler waited in vain for his daughter's return. When she did not arrive he went to the shop, but found it locked up and silent. He went to the Midland station, but it was deserted, and finally, he went to Burton's lodgings to ask if he knew anything about his daughter's disappearance. Burton was staying with Mr Butler's wife's cousin, a man called Benjamin Cook, at 17 Gloucester Crescent. Butler told his relative that his daughter had left home, and that he didn't know where she had gone. When the distraught father asked to speak to Burton, Cook went upstairs to wake Burton – but Burton refused to answer the door. Finally Cook told Butler to return the following day. Something about the events caused Cook to be suspicious, however, and after Butler had gone Cook woke him and asked him if he knew anything about the disappearance of Miss Butler. Burton admitted that he had helped her to find new lodgings after she told him that she 'lived in fear of her father'. They went to the lodgings of Mr Mirfin and there found Miss Butler. Cook told her that her father had been looking for her and advised her to go home, but she didn't answer him. Still keeping up the pretence that they were just work colleagues, Burton asked her to go home to her father. Once again she refused.

On the return journey to his own lodgings, Burton finally confessed to Cook that he was a widower and that he wanted to marry Miss Butler – but her father, he said, would not agree to the marriage, and so she was staying at the lodgings until he could make arrangements for them to wed. He did not state at any time that the couple planned to elope. At sometime between 2 a.m. and 3 a.m., Burton arrived at Alderson Road and woke Miss Burton, saying that there had been a change of plan. He told her that instead of getting married in Sheffield they should leave the town and get married somewhere else. Enquiring at the station, he was told that the first train out of the station was to Leicester at 4 a.m. and he bought tickets for them both. Mr Butler continued looking for his daughter and on Sunday 2 October returned to Cook's house; Cook told him that Burton had left the house sometime during the night. Mr Butler finally realised what the scheming couple were up to when he discovered that his daughter had also left her new lodgings in the early hours of the morning. Butler reported his daughter missing to the police, and it was not long before they told him that their enquiries had shown that Burton's wife and two children were still very much alive. It was not until Wednesday 5 October that the police told him that they had tracked the couple to Leicester.

On Saturday 8 October Mr Butler, accompanied by Police Constable Nelson, went to Leicester to find them. They had previously contacted the Leicester

Alderson Road.

Fargate Road, where Miss Butler lived with her father.

Above left: Entrance to Midland station in 1870.

Above right: Unidentified policeman, late nineteenth century.

police and discovered that the pair had been living in a house on Ashwell Street. A detective from the Leicester police force accompanied them to the house at 1 p.m. and found the couple there. Miss Burton told her father that they had been married the previous day at Belvoir Street Chapel and showed him her wedding ring. Mr Butler told her that her marriage was illegal because Burton was already married. She refused to believe her father, and was not convinced until she returned to Sheffield and the fact was confirmed by the police authorities there. In a separate room, Burton was at that moment confessing to Police Constable Nelson that they had indeed been married the day before. When confronted with the truth, Burton also admitted that he was already married. He had married his first wife, Mary, on 26 May 1877 at the Church of St Clements at Sheepscar in Leeds. After the marriage, the pair had lived with her father at Roundhay Road, Leeds; when Burton got a job at Mr Butler's in August 1877, the pair moved to Sheffield. After he had served his sentence for robbery, they had moved to Rotherham and from there to a place near Barnsley. In January of 1879 he had abandoned his young child and his wife whilst she was nursing her six-week-old baby. He told Police Constable Nelson that his wife had been fortunate to get herself a teaching job in a board school in Chesterfield, where she lived with the two children. But before he married Miss Butler, he had made arrangements to meet his wife and his two children at Chesterfield station on 1 October – though he doubtless did not inform her of his forthcoming nuptials.

On Wednesday 13 October, Burton was brought back to Sheffield, and he appeared before the magistrates the next day, charged with bigamy. Annie Elizabeth Butler gave evidence. She spoke about getting to know Burton when he first went to work for her father in August 1877; she knew on that occasion that he was a married man. She described how he told her sad stories of the death of his wife – and how he had only been in the post for three weeks when he first asked her to marry him. She had made no reply on that occasion but he persisted, demanding she elope with him, until finally she gave in. The original plan had been to marry in Sheffield and then travel to his mother's house at Normanton. (No doubt his mother would have been very surprised when he arrived with his new bride, so it is probable that he was lying to her about their destination.) She was startled when he arrived in the early hours of the morning at Alderson Road and informed her that her father had been to the house on Gloucester Crescent, and was planning to return in the morning; they then travelled to the station in the early hours and on to Leicester. They had lodged in a Temperance Hotel where they had stayed for two or three days before being married on 7 October 1880. So compelling was her testimony that the jury took very little time to consider the case and found him guilty. He was sent for trial at the Assizes.

Burton was tried at the Leeds Assizes on Friday 5 November 1880. His defence could only suggest that Burton was very young, and that, at twenty-three years of age, the judge might look leniently on him. Unfortunately, the judge did not agree with this view. Passing sentence, he told him:

> This case is the worst case of bigamy I have tried. I hope that I never have to try another one like it. You were taken into the confidence of your master. He took you into his house and he gave you food, shelter and employment. What was the return you made to him? You, a married man, seduced his daughter by pretending you were able to marry her and took her away from her father's house and made her a disgrace to him for ever. I pass on you the severest sentence I have ever passed before.

He then sentenced him to eighteen months in prison with hard labour. Given that the usual prison term for bigamy was six months, this was a very harsh sentence indeed.

Yet twenty years earlier a more serious bigamy case had been heard before the Assizes in Sheffield, when Harry Lloyd Bickerstaff, aged thirty-four, pleaded guilty to marrying Anna Marie Campbell whilst his former wife, Mona Brougham Bickerstaff, was still alive and living in Leeds. Bickerstaff, who was the son of a clergyman, had lived in one of the Midland counties. In 1850, whilst studying at St Bee's Theological College in Cumberland, he met his first wife, Miss Mona Brougham Drew, the daughter of Revd P.W. Drew, the rector of Youghall, County Cork, in Ireland. After twelve months' courtship, they were married at Youghall with the blessings of both families. After holding several curacies, the prisoner went to Headingley in Leeds, where his habits 'became irregular'. After leaving home in 1859 nothing more was heard of him, until a paragraph appeared in *The Times* of 11 October 1859 announcing the marriage of the Revd Bickerstaff at Barlow near Linton in Cambridgeshire to Miss Anna Marie Campbell, a lady who, it was said, possessed a legacy of £5,000 in her own right. It appeared that after leaving Headingley he obtained a curacy under the Revd Henry Blanker, an incumbent of Godalming in Surrey, and there became engaged to Miss Campbell. Shortly afterwards he tumbled off the rector's coach in a state of intoxication – and, as a consequence of this behaviour, was ejected from the Rectory. Miss Campbell was made aware of the circumstances but nonetheless forgave him, and the arrangements for the marriage went ahead. It took place on 15 October at Brighton. Possibly Miss Campbell was beginning to wonder about the steadiness of her husband-to-be even on that great day – for Bickerstaff failed to show up. A dinner for sixty persons had been arranged with all the trimmings. When he did finally arrive, the ever-patient Miss Campbell forgave him and a private, smaller ceremony took place. The happy couple lived together for just a fortnight before Miss Campbell was informed by her brother that Bickerstaff was a married man, and that a warrant for his arrest had been taken out. Before he was apprehended, however, he fled to Rhyl (where he was later arrested).

The Campbell family appears as a whole to have had a very forgiving nature: Miss Campbell's brother, Archibald Samuel Campbell, appeared at the Assizes to reassure the court that Miss Campbell had not instigated the present proceedings. He tried to excuse Bickerstaff's behaviour by telling the jury that he felt that Bickerstaff was of a weak mind and perhaps was not always aware of his actions. But the judge was not so forgiving: in fact, he was incensed that Bickerstaff, a clergyman, could commit such a crime. He told the prisoner that his offence was one of the most aggravated nature: 'as a clergyman of the Church of England and a man of education you wilfully married knowing that your wife was still alive. You committed a deep injury to a young woman and an outrage to society. I feel obliged to pass a sentence that you will feel with double the severity of ordinary criminals.' He then sentenced him to penal servitude for three years.

Harsh sentences were an attempt by the legal system to dissuade people from committing bigamy. However, on some occasions it seems that bigamous couples made private arrangements to accommodate themselves.

Ann Birkhead had married her husband George on 18 July 1836, and they set up home in Brightside, Sheffield. Many years later she was deserted by her husband, and, as often happened in this era, was forced to provide her own living as best she could. In either July or August 1839 her husband returned to Sheffield and she resumed living with him. She had been keeping house for a Mr Jessop at

Elsecar whilst he had been away. It seems that George Birkhead was not thrilled with this arrangement, and told her that she 'had better get Jessop to marry her if he would'. He even went so far as to give his wife a formal document stating that he gave his permission for her to marry Jessop. Mr Jessop appears to have been quite amenable to the idea, for the marriage took place on 19 September 1839. At the beginning of 1840 the matter was brought to the attention of the police force and she was brought before the magistrate. The magistrates found her guilty and sent her for trial at the Assizes. When the subject of bail was agreed, the case took on a comic turn: bail was offered by both Birkhead and Jessop.

At the trial on Thursday 11 March 1840, the judge told the court that this was one of the most curious cases he had had before him since sitting on the judicial bench – he could not understand why the charge had been brought. He called the police officer who had apprehended the prisoner, who told the learned judge that the woman was given in charge to him by the Revd Cummings. His Lordship remarked that he supposed Mr Cummings had been taking care of the morals of his parish, but thought he might have employed his time better than in instigating the prosecution at present before them. The judge then ordered that the reverend gentleman be telegraphed so that the court might be put into possession of 'his grounds for interfering in the matter'. On the following day, Mr Cummings duly arrived and gave a long and rambling explanation of events. He stated that the new Mrs Jessop had visited him in order to try to get Jessop, who was worth in the region of £100-£200, to leave his money to her when he died. His Lordship felt that Cummings had wasted the court's time. He stated that: 'The prosecution was an unwarranted one and it was not required in the interests of morality or on any other grounds. He much regretted the want of care on the part of the magistrates in sending such a case for trial'.

His Lordship added that he should give the prisoner the slightest punishment in his power and should show his opinion of the prosecution and the interference of Mr Cummings by refusing costs to both. He sentenced Mrs Birkhead/Jessop to one month's imprisonment. It seems that if both parties agreed to the marriage and the husband gave permission, it was not a heinous crime.

Chapter Six

✴ INCEST AND INFANTICIDE ✴

adly, the life of working-class women in Victorian Sheffield was more often than not an unhappy one. Single women were usually subject to their parents' will, and there was little in the way of work for them to do. Many chose a life of domestic service, often a life of drudgery and hard work. As we have already seen, the morality of the period was a strict one, and if a single woman became pregnant she was supposed to be at fault. The man who impregnated her would not be seen as culpable. The poor desperate girls who found themselves in such a condition had few options available: either they could carry the child to term, and both mother and child would be castigated for as long as they lived, or they could rid themselves of the problem one way or another. I have no doubt that there were many abortionists in the back streets of Sheffield who, for a small charge, would release the girl from her dilemma. If the poor woman had no money at all, she sometimes had no option but to rid herself of the child after it was born. Some chose to murder the child; others abandoned it in the river or elsewhere. Several times every year there were discoveries of the bodies of newly born infants abandoned by their mothers. It almost seems that death was a form of birth control for some poor women who had no other alternative. Sometimes, and we have no idea how common this was, a baby would die from being given indigestible food, as in this next case. There was no counselling available and little thought was given to the mental health of a woman driven to pursue such actions, or who lost a child. The following cases indicate the opprobrium that was felt towards such a woman, and sometimes towards their families too.

This first case of an illegitimate birth was discussed in the local newspaper, and the disgust of the people in the town led a family to be excommunicated from the Catholic faith, cursed from the pulpit, and resulted in a riot. The riot had been instigated by some members of the Catholic faith who should have been in a position to offer charity and forgiveness. Historically, respectable citizens of many towns looked down on Irish Catholics, many of whom had flooded into the city from the port of Liverpool following the potato failures in Ireland between 1845 and 1852. Many rented houses and places of employment had signs stating 'No Irish need apply'. So the details of this crime were widely reported in the local newspapers of the time. Following an inquest held at the Sheffield Workhouse on

Wednesday 31 October 1860, reports were published containing 'details of the disgusting immorality and the means taken by some of the priesthood of the Roman Catholic Church to show their abhorrence of such proceedings'.

'Disgusting morality' was a reference to the case's unusual background: the child had been born out of incest. An inquest was held on the body of a female child 'nine days old' that had died on the evening of Monday 29 October. The mother of the child was called Mary Sheardon, and she lived with her mother on Pea Croft. Mary's mother's paramour was a man called Dominic Larvin, an Irish labourer aged forty-five, who stayed at the house for a number of years as her husband and was reported as being the father of the child. The couple had two children. Mary Sheardon was the only daughter and when she attained the age of fifteen in June 1860, she began to be unwell. Her mother, who was unaware – or pretended to be unaware – of her daughter's condition, took her to the Infirmary. The surgeon, realising the girl's plight, refused to have anything to do with her, and she was forced to return home – where a fortnight later she gave birth to a baby. When this information reached the ears of Father Kennedy, the family's Catholic priest at St Vincent's Church, he cursed the family from the pulpit during Mass on 28 October. He announced to the shocked congregation that he had excommunicated the mother, father, the girl and the child. He must have been particularly incensed, as following this condemnation he went to the house at midnight on the same evening and demanded to be allowed to enter. Fear of the Catholic priest was prevalent in many – if not most – Irish Catholic families at the time, which ensured that he would be given entrance. Whilst in the house, he took hold of a plaster statue of Jesus Christ and smashed it to the floor, telling Sheardon's mother that she was not worthy to have it in the house – and then he struck her on the side of her face with his open hand. It was reported, although the reporter admitted that he could not vouch for the accuracy of details, that Kennedy then cursed the house and called upon all faithful Catholics to do the same. Regretfully, the report appears to have been true, as the family had 'a great commotion' outside the house for the rest of the night.

The following night the mob was outside again, and began to throw bricks at the windows. Mary told the police that some of the mob were members of a society called the Young Men's Society, as well as other Catholics of the neighbourhood. She also told them that so many bricks had been thrown that all the beds upstairs in the house were covered in them. The mob proceeded to break open the doors of the house; it was estimated that 200 people were gathered outside. Twenty police constables were dispatched to the area to try to maintain order. It seems that they managed, after a struggle, to prevent the mob entering the house. No doubt had they not succeeded then the inmates would have been seriously hurt, perhaps even killed.

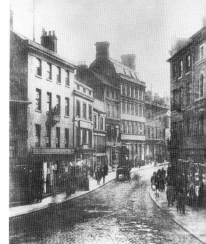

Above left: Entrance to Pea Croft.

Above centre: Housing in Campo Lane where Larvin took refuge.

Above right: Clarence Hotel, High Street.

One of the constables, Edward Shaw, knew the high regard in which most Catholics held their priests, and had begged one of them to come to the house to quell the mob; he declined, stating that the Sheardon family 'were not worthy of their [the priesthood's] protection'. When the attack started again on the Monday evening, Mary was lying on the sofa in the kitchen with the baby in a rocking chair surrounded by cushions. The baby had been subject to convulsions which had started on the Saturday. Mary's mother went upstairs to try to identify anyone in the mob and when she returned back downstairs found the rocking chair had been tipped over by a brick. The child was not injured by the brick, but nevertheless died that evening between the hours of 11 p.m. and 12 p.m.

The father of the baby, Larvin, took refuge on the Tuesday at a house in Campo Lane, but once the attack started again on the Tuesday evening and his whereabouts became known, the mob attacked the house where he was staying as well as the family home in Pea Croft. It was reported that although the house had suffered greatly at the hands of the mob, the attack on Tuesday was less severe than it had been, and this was probably due to the baby's death. Unfortunately rumours began to circulate that the child had been poisoned, and so it was felt necessary to hold an inquest. Sheardon, for her own safety, had been taken to the Sheffield Workhouse, and it was there that the inquest was held. The surgeon, Mr Booth, and Mr Skinner, the Medical Officer of the workhouse, held a post mortem and found that the baby had died through natural causes. Mr Booth had treated the child for convulsions on the evening that it had died. They found that death was caused by congestion of the brain through administration of indigestible food. The jury was directed to give a verdict according to the medical evidence and the girl was dismissed.

From our modern perspective, the whole situation was handled in a dreadful and horrifying manner. For the family to be subjected to such behaviour by a Catholic priest defies belief. An illegitimate birth is no longer viewed with the horror it was in Victorian times. But this case does graphically indicate the horror felt towards a woman who gave birth to an illegitimate child.

The following case is another involving an Irish woman. Mary Loughman was a native of Tipperary who came to Britain in January 1878. She gained employment with a Mrs Leticia Susannah Matthews as a domestic servant of Brookhill, Sheffield. She remained there until September 1878, when she left to take up a position of kitchen maid at the Clarence Hotel in the High Street. For whatever reason, she returned to the service of Mrs Matthews at the beginning of May 1879. She appeared to have put on quite a lot of weight, but when suggestions were made to her that she might be pregnant she denied them. Miss Matthews was so convinced that she was pregnant that she asked Dr Edward Skinner to examine her on 22 May, which he did. He found that she had very recently been confined – he estimated as recently as the previous day – and he asked her where the baby was; still she denied having given birth to a child. He called the next day and told her that he thought she looked ill. Still denying that she had given birth, she left the house rather hurriedly. A short time later, a very disagreeable smell filled the house of Miss Matthews. At first she dismissed it as the drain, but after a while the smell could not be ignored. On 15 June she sent for the police to investigate.

Police Constable Thornton and Police Constable Walton arrived at the house the following day and started their search. The worst stench was coming from the area of the cellar, and upon investigation they narrowed it down to the top of the cellar step – where they found the remains of a boy child secreted under the boards at the top of the steps. To their horror, they discovered that the body had been dismembered into five pieces. Mr Hallam, a surgeon at the Sheffield Infirmary, examined the remains and gave his opinion: the child, he declared, was born alive and had had a separate existence from the mother. It was a fully developed male child with no marks of cutting – the limbs had been torn from the body (which I feel indicates the absolute desperation of the mother). He gave his opinion that the limbs had been torn after the child had died, but when asked if he could judge how the baby had died he said that there were many reason for a newly born child to die. However, after taking a statement from Miss Matthews they arrested Miss Loughman at her new place of employment in Ashdell Road (where she was once again in service). She was arrested on a charge of murder, brought before the magistrates on 25 June 1879, found guilty and sent to the Assizes.

Loughman was brought to the Assizes on Wednesday 30 July 1879, and the evidence was heard against her. Mr Hallam's evidence pointed to the fact that the child could have died from many causes. The judge concurred, and felt that this was not a case of murder; the charge was therefore reduced to that of 'concealing the birth of a child'. The judge told Loughman:

> Whether you did or did not murder your child is known only to yourself. The circumstances are such as to leave the highest suspicion and manner in which you behaved to the dead body of your own offspring. Even if the child did die a natural death you have shown yourself an unnatural mother. I don't know about murder and I don't want to know. It is my duty to pass on you a sentence which will mark the sense which the court entertains of the absence of all natural feeling and its determination to severely punish those who try to hide their shame by an act of brutal cruelty and bring upon themselves a dual and triple sense of infamy.

The poor girl was then sentenced to eighteen months' imprisonment with hard labour.

The next case, which took place in March 1847, shook the town, not so much by the fact that it had happened, but by the manner of the disposal of the body – it was found hidden in night soil. Night soil is a Victorian description for the contents of the privy. At the beginning of the century drainage was very basic, and toilets would consist of ash pits over which seating was arranged, the matter falling into a pit which night-soil men would then empty. This was a thankless job (and, in the days of very little sanitation, a very dangerous one as all sorts of diseases could be caught). On Tuesday night, 2 March, at approximately 2 a.m., the men were working in a private yard owned by Messrs Ridall and Allwood of Market Street, when the shovel of one of the workmen, David Hague, hit something – a shape which, he thought, was a dead dog wrapped in bed ticking. (Ticking is traditionally striped material that was used to cover mattresses and pillows.) It was very dark in the yard, so placing the mass on his shovel he threw it into the cart used to remove the night soil and pushed the cart out into the street. The cart was then removed to the premises of Mr Spooner of Templar Street at about 6.30 a.m. when George Handley spotted the bundle. He noted the ticking first, and, when he went to open it, he realised by the smell that it was a decomposing body and the police were called. Police Constable Joseph Valentine went to the site at Market Street to look at the yard where the baby had been found. He noted that it was a private yard with no thoroughfare for people other than those employed at the house of Mr Ridall. Handley told Valentine that the privy had been emptied four months previously. To place the body where it was found would have entailed someone squeezing through a three-foot high door or throwing the little body over a fence. He then went to Templar Street and saw the body, which was by now laid in the road. He took the tiny bundle to the Town Hall where both the body and the material it was wrapped in were washed. Alongside the ticking was some material made out of calico which had been wrapped around the baby's head.

It was agreed that an inquest would be held on the body the following day in front of the coroner Mr T. Badger. In the meantime, the police would make enquiries in order to find the mother of the child. A surgeon had examined the body and told the inquest that he felt that whoever had given birth to the child had no medical knowledge, as the umbilical cord, instead of being tied, had been cut close to the baby's body. He had examined the body externally and found no bruises or marks on it which would indicate the way the baby had died, nor if it breathed and therefore had a separate existence to the mother.

It seems that the following day a young woman was suspected of having given birth to the child. She was a servant of Mr Ridall named Sarah Drabble and had been in his service for eighteen months as a kitchen maid.

Night soil cart on West Street, 1913.

High Street and Market Street.

Drabble had appeared to be happy in her work at Mr Charles Ridall's. Drabble was supervised by Mrs Elizabeth Marshall, the under-housekeeper for Mr Ridall. She was described as being about twenty-two years of age and a very good worker. The under-housekeeper noted that about September or October 1846 she had looked ill and she noted that she was stouter than was usual. When Marshall asked her if she was feeling well, she told her that she was. Marshall had a pretty good idea of what the matter was, but, with Victorian sensibilities, asked her if anything was wrong. She insisted that she was quite well. During the following month of November, Marshall again commented that Drabble looked pale and poorly: she told Marshall that she was suffering from a bowel complaint, and had been poorly the previous night. Taking the bull by the horns, Marshall at last asked her if she was in 'the family way'. Drabble denied it. Marshall gave her some brandy and peppermint and sent her back to bed. She was very surprised to see the girl an hour and a half later. Drabble said that she was feeling much better and she continued with her duties serving at the family dinner table. Marshall's acute eyesight saw a girl who was thinner than she had been previously. When news got out about a baby being found, Marshall spoke to her employer Mr Ridall about her suspicions, and Drabble was sent for. He told Drabble in the presence of the housekeeper that she had to go to the Town Hall and see the Chief Constable Mr Raynor and confess. Drabble told him that she knew nothing about a baby, stating categorically, 'I have not had a child and I know nothing about it.'

At the inquest, held the following day, Marshall told the jury that she had kept some ticking whilst in the service of Mr Ridall for wiping the iron and to use as a duster; it was kept in a drawer to which all the servants had access. It was some months since she had seen the ticking and prior to the inquest had searched high and low for it, but it had gone. Marshall was shown the piece of ticking found with the dead baby and she identified it as the one used at the house. Drabble's sister, who had also worked at the house since 1 September 1846, and who shared a bed with her sister, told the coroner that she knew nothing about a baby, nor had she seen the ticking which Marshall had identified. The terrified Drabble was brought into the inquest and was cautioned that she needn't make a statement unless she wanted to. Without the oath being administered, she told the court that she knew nothing about a baby's body until the previous evening when Mr Ridall informed her of the gruesome discovery. She had previously suffered from a bowel complaint and was ill on the days that Marshall had spoken about, a complaint brought about, she thought, by the late nights she worked whilst caring for Mr Ridall's partner (who had since died). The surgeon gave evidence and stated that in his opinion the child was approximately two months old, but he could confirm it better after he had completed a post mortem. This was agreed, and the inquest was adjourned until Friday.

At the adjourned inquest, the surgeon told the coroner and the jury that the child had been born approximately twelve weeks before. The jury took no time in finding Drabble guilty of wilful murder, and the coroner sentenced her for trial at the next Assizes. It seems that by the time of the trial in May 1847, Drabble had suffered a great deal emotionally, as it was reported that although only twenty-three she looked at least ten years older. The judge, after hearing the evidence, once again asked that the capital charge be dismissed. He requested that Drabble be charged with the lesser crime of 'concealment of birth'. The girl sobbed throughout the evidence against her, and more so whilst Marshall repeated her claims. The judge appeared to take a more lenient view of the matter, for he sentenced her to six months' imprisonment. Drabble, if guilty, might have got off fairly lightly in her sentencing, but nevertheless the fact that a child's body had been found in night soil had shocked Sheffield society. The newspapers of the time hold regular reports of dead babies being found in all sorts of places, but the manner of disposal in this case was unusually offensive, and appalled the reading public. Once again this case underlines the sense of panic which grips a girl who is forced to destroy the evidence of her transgression.

Chapter Seven

'ONLY FOOLS AND HORSES WORK'

This phrase, for many years associated with a wonderful comedy series featuring David Jason and Nicholas Lyndhurst, appears to be older than at first thought. This saying was used in the Victorian period, and is spoken by one of the main protagonists in the next case – but that, alas, is where the similarity ends. This crime was very violent and distasteful, and if not for the resourcefulness of a very brave woman could have resulted in death for the whole family and their two domestic servants.

There were several breweries in and around Sheffield in the nineteenth century, and most were very successful businesses – and, as a consequence, a target for criminals. One such brewery owner was Mr William Bradley. When he returned to his home on Eyre Street at 8 p.m. on the night of 8 December 1856, he counted the takings for the day as soon as he had had his supper. He counted £30-£40 in gold sovereigns and three £5 notes (known as 'Doncaster notes'). These had a very distinct design and one was rather dirty. His wife, Mrs Charlotte Bradley, wanted some money from her husband and when she asked him if he could let her have some, he told her 'no'; she picked up the dirty £5 note and asked him if she could have that instead, but he returned it to his pocket. The family consisted of the couple, Mrs Bradley's mother (who was staying with her daughter as she was very ill) and two other maidservants. Due to her mother's illness, Charlotte Bradley was forced to either share the same bed as her mother, or to sleep in the dressing room to be closer to her should she cry out in the middle of the night. There were also other menservants who lived in some adjacent property. The couple retired to bed about midnight, and Mrs Bradley went into the adjoining dressing room after saying 'goodnight' to her husband.

Shortly after 2 a.m., Mrs Bradley was awoken by the sound of breaking glass and she went into her husband's bedroom where she found him asleep. Crying 'William, William,' she woke him. No sooner had he sat up than five men dashed into the bedroom: two of the men were wearing cotton masks with eye holes, both of which were quite tight at the top of the head, but one of the men's masks was looser at the bottom, revealing a little of his face. The other men had blackened their faces in an attempt not to be recognised. One was carrying a revolver belonging to Mr Bradley and the other a life-preserver (a stick or baton which is weighted at one end). Another man was holding a candle which Bradley recognised as coming from downstairs, and the other a dark lantern. They rushed to the bed and attacked Mr Bradley with fists and blows from the life-preserver. He ran into a corner of the room and made himself as small as possible. The men still rained down blows on him and his brave wife stood in front of him, trying to prevent any further attacks. The men were shouting 'Damn him!' and 'Murder him!' whilst attacking. One blow missed and hit his wife on the bosom with such a force that she thought she was going to faint. Another violent blow broke two fingers of Bradley's hand.

After about fifteen minutes of violence, one of them said 'Spare her, she's a good sort'. Another demanded Bradley's money. He replied that the money was in his trouser pocket, and gave the men his trousers. They took the money out and shouted at him to tell them where the rest of it was. One of them tried to jemmy open some drawers in the bedroom. Bradley told them, 'If you want my property, use the keys,' and gave them the keys to the drawers. They went through all the drawers and took several brooches and some old coins. They also took a gold watch belonging to Bradley from the top of the drawers; Mrs Bradley handed it to them, noting that it was 2.30 a.m. At the same time it crossed her mind that she might be able to leap out of the bedroom window and raise the alarm, but as she glanced out she saw two men outside, one wearing what she described as a billy cock hat, keeping guard. The men continued to attack Mr Bradley, shouting and blaspheming and saying, 'Kill the old rascal'.

The five men then went to the room recently vacated by Mrs Bradley, and one was heard to cry 'hey lads, this is the shop', as they found that Bradley used the room in which to store his silver. They took three silver tea pots, two silver sugar basins, thirty-six tea spoons, twelve silver forks and one silver-plated sugar basket, as well as another gold watch belonging to Mrs Bradley. They next moved towards the bedroom of Mrs Bradley's mother. She begged them not to disturb the old lady, who was very ill and close to death. One of the men looked into the room and then withdrew without entering. They next went to the servant's quarters where they found two young women sleeping in the same bed. One of the men grabbed one of the girls by her hair, swearing that he would kill her if she did not lie still. He demanded any money that they might have, but the girl told him they had none. The other girl, who buried herself beneath the covers, said nothing as the men went through their boxes. Finding nothing, they then went back to Bradley's bedroom. Threatening the couple with violence if they raised the alarm, the men went downstairs and left the house through the front door (which had been left open for this very purpose). Bradley found that the shutters to the dining room had been forced and this was how the men had made their entry.

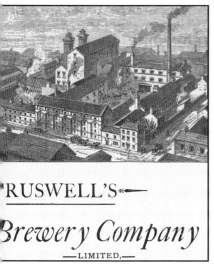

Above left: Truswell's Brewery, Eyre Street.

Above right: Silver bowl and cups similar to those stolen in the robbery, *c.* 1930.

Main Road, Darnall, 1930.

On leaving the house, the men went towards Darnall, going over the Don Bridge at Brightside to Ecclesfield and thence to Barnsley. (This rather circuitous route ensured that they would stay on the back roads and avoid any confrontation with police constables who might be patrolling the area.) Nevertheless, they were spotted by several witnesses who gave evidence at their trial. One of these witnesses was a woman named Sarah Underwood, who was a hawker by trade. She saw a man whom she knew called Marsden prowling about with six others on the morning of the robbery, and noted that four of them were at the same spot in the evening looking over the wall of the house belonging to Bradley. Two of these men she knew as Dickenson, aged thirty-six, and Gledall, aged thirty-five; the other two she was not sure of. She told the constable that Dickenson was from Rawmarsh near Rotherham, and that Gledall lived at Barnsley. Only Marsden was a local man: he lived quite near to Bradley's house, and it was noted that shortly after the robbery he moved to Hampden View on the other side of Sheffield. Another witness, William Cheetham, saw the seven men come past where he was standing by the Globe Inn on Howard Street; they went in the direction of Brightside Bridge over the Don. In total, seven witnesses swore that they had seen the group of men on their way to Barnsley on the night of the robbery.

The Globe, Howard Street.

Meanwhile, the men were spending freely. A landlady named Mary Foster, who kept a public house in Worsbrough Common, told the court that she knew Dickenson and that a few nights after the robbery he gave her a £5 Doncaster note that she described as being very dirty. She was shown the actual note and identified it as the one given to her by Dickenson. Benjamin Harrison, who kept the Omar Pasha Beerhouse (named after the General of the Ottoman Empire, now modern Turkey), noticed the men drinking in his pub after the robbery. He named the men as Dickenson, Gledall and Marsden; they were with George Gouldthorpe, Thomas Simpson and James Ewing, and they were all playing dominoes. Every time they came up to the bar for another round they proffered a gold sovereign. When someone asked out loud where the men got their money from, as none of them were in work, Dickenson replied, 'Only fools and horses work.' The fact that the men were seen spending freely naturally alerted the police and that, combined with the evidence of the witnesses, was enough to take them into custody. Sheffield Police Inspector Samuel Linley told the court that he went to Barnsley to arrest Dickenson; Linley told him that he had only been in Barnsley for half an hour, and had travelled there by luggage train. After further information was received, Gledall and Marsden were also arrested.

Mr and Mrs Bradley were asked separately if they could identify the men from an identity parade and were able to pick them out. Mr Bradley said that he recognised Dickenson as his mask had been flapping about at the bottom of his face – due to the ferocity of the attack she could see his lower face quite distinctly. He also told the court that he was in fear of his life during the attack as some of the men had cried out 'Murder him!' and 'We mean to murder the old rascal'. Mrs Bradley also identified Dickenson from the gap in his mask, and Gledall from his stature. This brave woman went up close to Gledall, and said, 'You see, you haven't quite killed us.' At this his face changed and he appeared to become more thoughtful. What she didn't know until later was that another person who was in custody with Dickenson and Gledall, a prisoner called Edward Wright, was sharing the exercise yard and heard Dickenson say to Gledall that next time he would not get the other lightly with a few scratches, but 'would have his jemmy croked'. Wright took this to mean that next time Dickenson would make sure that no witnesses were left to identify him.

At the York Assizes in February 1857 Mrs Bradley, when giving evidence, told the court how she had tried to protect her husband from some of the blows. She had tried to take the life-preserver away from one of the men but saw that it was strapped to his wrist, and knew that she would be unable to do so. The court heard the sound of someone clapping the bravery of Mrs Bradley, but the judge, Mr Baron Martin, ordered the applause to stop, saying, 'if anyone does that again they will be brought before me and sent to prison,' reminding them that this was a court of justice. Inspector Linley had visited the house where the robbery took place and, in true Sherlock Holmes' style, found a boot print in the flowerbeds near to the house. He placed a roof tile over the mark to preserve it and requested another Inspector, Ephraim Sills, to collect the boots belonging to Gledall (who had been arrested at his sister's house in Barnsley on 18 December, and who was now in the cells at the Town Hall). When compared, the boots fitted the print perfectly. The same day, Marsden was arrested; on searching him Sills found a parcel containing the two gold watches stolen from the house, and he gave them into the custody of Superintendent Raynor. Marsden told him that he had found the gold watches at the back of where he lived on Hampden View. At the trial, Mr Raynor showed the watches, and Mrs Bradley identified them as belonging to herself and her husband and asked the judge if she might have them back. The judge could see no reason why she could not have them back, and light-heartedly she took them from him. Unfortunately her triumph was short lived – she tripped and fell whilst leaving the witness box and had to be lifted up by one of the court ushers.

Sarah Underwood told the jury about seeing the men hanging around the Bradleys' house on the day of the robbery, and also told them about what happened when she went to identify Marsden: the police had taken her to a window overlooking the prisoners in the yard below and, before she could speak, Marsden had looked up at her and shouted, 'Don't know me mistress, go home.' She identified him nonetheless.

The judge summed up the case for the jury. He told them that if they agreed with the evidence then they had to give a guilty verdict, but if any reasonable doubt should be given they must acquit them. The jury retired at 11.45 a.m. and left the court to make their verdict, leaving the prisoners sitting in the court with a gaoler on either side of them all. It was noted that Dickenson and Gledall spoke softly to each other during the jury's absence, but neither man spoke to Marsden. After an absence of nearly two hours the jury returned a verdict of guilty of burglary and violence against all three prisoners. Mr Baron Martin gave the sentence that all three men would be 'transported across the seas for the term of their natural life'. The gaolers were just about to put on the manacles to take them across the castle yard to the prison when Dickenson burst into tears, crying, 'I am going away an innocent man.' The judge told him, 'As far as my judgment goes the verdict is a fair one.' Gledall, striking the crown of his hat as he put it on in order to accompany the gaolers to prison, shouted out, 'I hope the real men come forward and then we will see whether you are right or not.'

This was a very brutal and ferocious attack on the people in the Bradley household. The prisoners made it very clear that they would not hesitate to murder the victims should there be a next time. They appeared to be men with little compassion, and the heroism of Mrs Bradley deserved more than a round of applause in the court room.

Chapter Eight

GARROTTING ROBBERIES

In the years between 1854 and 1860 there were a series of 'garrotte robberies' in the streets of Sheffield. Garrotting was a method of strangulation using string, wire or cord around the neck of the victim. However, these robbers used a slightly different method: strong and powerful hands were held to the throat, preventing the victim from crying out, whilst a partner robbed the helpless victim of their possessions. The force used to control the victim would have made it very dangerous – and very easy to actually kill the person. But why garroting became such a popular crime in Sheffield during these years was a mystery. One answer might be that most of the victims were attacked from behind, and therefore their attackers generally remained out of sight; in almost every case at least one of the perpetrators remained at large, possibly due to this. Those that were identified were usually caught when the victim recognised their voices or their general gait.

Joseph White was a Sheffield smith, a striker by trade. On the night of 11 December 1859 he met his wife at about 9.30 p.m. and they walked home together. Approaching the Lord Raglan public house on Bridge Street, he asked his wife to return home and make his supper, while he went into the pub and ordered a pint of ale. He did not notice three men – one known as Thomas Russell, aged twenty-three – watching him as he took out his silver watch to check the time. The landlady of the pub saw the three men follow White outside when he left. He walked briskly along Mill Lane towards his home – and, when he was within twenty yards of the safety of his house, the men struck. They attacked him by seizing his throat and pulling him to the floor. Searching through his pockets they found the silver watch and took it. They demanded money from White; he told them that he did not have any, and eventually they ran away. The following day, White attended an identity parade at the Town Hall to try to pick his attacker out of a line up, but he was unable to identify him with any certainty. However, the landlady of the Lord Raglan had no such qualms, and readily identified Russell as being one of the men who had left the public house just after White had gone out the door. A further (unnamed) witness stated that they had seen Russell near to the place where the robbery had taken place. Russell was found guilty and sent to the Assizes. When the case was heard on 8 March 1860, the defence tried to maintain that he had been wrongly identified, but the jury were convinced: they found him guilty, and he was sentenced to four years' penal servitude. The identity of the two accomplices was never established, and if it had not been for the identification of the landlady, Russell would have gone free.

Four of the most notorious garrote robbers in Sheffield during this period were William Burkinshaw, aged twenty, Thomas Gould, nineteen, Henry Smith, eighteen, and James Lomas, twenty-three. No doubt the police had their names on file and they were investigated, but very little evidence could be brought against them. Burkinshaw and Smith were tried at the Winter Assizes of 1853, accused of robbing a young girl in Cavendish Street, but escaped conviction on that occasion. It was reported that they were suspected of committing a series of public house robberies in the town at the beginning of 1854. But it was not until 30 April that the police were able to establish that they had been involved in the garrote robbery of Mrs Mary Hibbert. Mary owned two grocer's shops, one in Cemetery Road and the other on Sheffield Moor. On the evening of 29 April, one of the men went into the shop on Sheffield Moor and asked for an ounce of tobacco. She served him, giving him the change from a tin in which she kept her cash. Whilst giving him the change, she saw him looking at the tin and trying to estimate how much money was in it. He then left the shop. On closing the shop at midnight, Mrs Hibbert locked up the shop, taking with her a leather pouch containing £16 in gold and silver, and, accompanied by her servant girl, Miss Lucy Ritchie, made her way home. On arriving at Cemetery Road, two men sprang at her; one, who she identified as Burkinshaw, seized her by the throat so that she could not cry out, and threw her to the ground, whilst two other men grabbed the servant girl, throwing her down to the ground also. Another man, who Mrs Hibbert identified as Lomas, then searched her pockets and her bosom and then, spying the leather pouch, made off with it. She noted that the man later identified as Gould held the servant girl Ritchie down with another man who she did not know at all. Although the night was dark and the nearest street lamp was thirty yards away, both Hibbert and Ritchie identified three of the men.

A witness, one Sarah Smith, who was on her way home with her husband at 1 a.m. on Cemetery Road, had also spotted the four men. The men pushed against her roughly and she gave that as a reason for noticing them particularly. Another witness, named Frost, reported seeing a man with a leather pouch jumping over a wall; he identified the man as Lomas. The leather pouch was found behind the same wall the following day by a police constable. Following Mrs Hibbert's statement at the Town Hall on 23 April, the police found that the men had gone to Manchester. Information was sent to the police there. Burkinshaw, Smith and Gould were found in Manchester on 9 May. They were hiding in an empty house and when the police

A court on Cavendish Street.

arrived they tried to make their escape, the prisoner Smith attempting to hide in a water butt outside. All three prisoners were escorted back to Sheffield.

One of the police superintendents from Manchester, a man named Patrick Shandley, was sent to assist the police in the capture of the four men. He was made responsible for getting Burkinshaw and Smith back to Sheffield and he secured seats on the train for that purpose. The two prisoners were handcuffed together and placed in a second-class carriage with Shandley sitting opposite them. Just before the Penistone Tunnel the two men started to act suspiciously and Shandley found that Smith had managed to free himself from his handcuffs: without speaking to each other the two prisoners set about Shandley, knocking him to the floor and beating him. At one point the carriage door flew open and they tried to push him out of the carriage, but Shandley fought back courageously. He shouted out to alert other people on the train but then saw Smith jumping out of the carriage door and disappearing. Once his companion had gone, Burkinshaw renewed his attack more ferociously, attacking Shandley with the handcuffs that were still attached to his wrists and crying, 'You had better let me go: I will take your life if you don't!' Shandley replied, 'You shall before I let you go.' Burkinshaw then attempted to drag Shandley out of the carriage, declaring that he would kill the both of them before he would let him go. Once again Shandley managed to hang on to the edge of the carriage door. Meanwhile the guard at the back of the train had spotted the open carriage door, and after emerging from the tunnel saw Burkinshaw attempting to get out of the carriage – only to be pulled back by someone inside. He heard a lot of shouting from the carriage, but was unable to attract the attention of the driver at the front of the train by waving a red flag.

A passing constable called Charles Beaumont witnessed Smith jumping from the train: he saw him land on his feet and then be pitched forward onto his head. He asked the stunned man why he had jumped from the train; Smith told him that he had been pushed out and that his brother and two of his sisters were on the train and had his ticket. The policeman did not believe him, and took him into custody. Meanwhile the train had stopped at last, and the guard and another gentleman went into the carriage. In it they found Shandley, partly lying on the seat, still holding fast to Burkinshaw. When he saw the two men, Burkinshaw finally gave in. The attack had been vicious, and Shandley collapsed; he was taken back to Sheffield where he was temporarily installed at the Hen & Chicken public house on Castlefolds to recover from his injuries. At Wortley, a railway police officer was put in the carriage with Shandley and his now subdued prisoner. Shandley, who had sustained some injuries in the struggle, was moaning quite loudly, and the railway police asked Burkinshaw why he had attacked him so fiercely. He answered, 'Never heed him if he dies. I would rather be hanged than transported.' Lomas was arrested. When taken into custody none of the prisoners had anything to say for themselves

Above left: Cemetery Road; Mrs Hibbert and her servant Lucy Ritchie were attacked here.

Above right: Hereford Street, 1920.

apart from Gould: he denied the charge, and claimed that on the night in question he had returned from Doncaster, and after a brief meeting with Smith and Lomas at the bottom of Hereford Street had bid them good night.

At the Assizes on 22 July 1854, the villains' defence lawyer tried to prove that the main witness, Mrs Hibbert, was in 'a state of terror' during the attack; consequently, he claimed, she was confused in her identification. The night had been very dark and because of this he demanded that no credence should be given to the witness. Though the fact that Burkinshaw had bought some tobacco on the night in question was irrefutable, there was no evidence against Gould at all. There was no case against Smith either, apart from the fact that he was captured with the other three men in Manchester. He requested the jury to dismiss all the charges, as it would be unsafe to prosecute the men on such flimsy evidence. The jury was not convinced, and after consultations lasting an hour found all four men guilty. The judge sentenced Gould and Lomas to fifteen years' transportation. The sentence against Burkinshaw and Smith was deferred as the two were to be tried for the other crime, that of the attempted murder of Patrick Shandley on 10 May 1854.

The long and hard struggle in the carriage was described, and the judge, in his summing up, told the jury that they had to decide whether there had been an intention to murder Shandley or whether the attack was simply to escape from his clutches. Smith had proved his case by escaping from the train, and he was acquitted; he was sentenced to six months' imprisonment for the robbery on Mrs Hibbert. Burkinshaw, however, had carried out a long and protracted attack on Shandley and suggested he would murder him if he could. The jury had no option but to find him guilty. The judge passed the sentence of death on him, adding that he should recommend to her Majesty that the sentence be reduced to transportation for life. His Lordship directed the High Sheriff to award Shandley £20 for his bravery, having discharged his duty faithfully under very difficult and trying circumstances and at the peril of his life.

No doubt it was a great relief to the officers of the Sheffield police force that these four brutal men were imprisoned. There seems little doubt that they had committed other crimes, probably other garroting crimes, on the streets of Sheffield.

Hen & Chickens public house, where Shandley recovered from his injuries.

Chapter Nine

THE FATHER-IN-LAW'S REVENGE

As we have already seen, immorality was considered an unforgivable offence in Victorian Sheffield. Crimes which smacked of fornication were labelled 'disgusting', and the double standards of the time ensured that woman were to be blamed for bringing any illegitimate child into the world. But the newspaper-buying public enjoyed reading about these kinds of crimes, which were endlessly sensationalised – and this next case was no exception. Terms such as the victim of 'incestuous lust and horrible revenge' were used to describe the events which led to this very sad event, which resulted in the deaths of both people involved.

Around noon on 6 December 1861, the sound of two pistol shots were heard in the vicinity of Carlisle Street East, Sheffield at the house of Mrs Travis. Mrs Travis lived with her son, John, and a young woman she had recently employed as her domestic servant. It seems that John had become smitten with this girl, whose name was Eliza Fisher; the servant was twenty years of age and described as a 'very fine young woman'. But this young woman was no innocent: she had been married previously, and then, about a year before this crime occurred, she had left her young husband to live with his father, a man reputed to be twice her age. His name was Thomas Townsend and he was a scissor maker of Attercliffe, once a beautiful rural area, but by 1861 a thriving industrial township. Matters were brought to a head when Eliza became pregnant and gave birth to a baby, who died shortly after. Filled with remorse at what she had done, Eliza left him and went to stay with an aunt, a Mrs Shepherd of Windsor Street. Townsend was not about to give up that easily: he visited her at her aunt's on two or three occasions in order to get her to go back to him, but she refused. She expressed her abhorrence of him to several people, and stated that she had no intention of returning to him.

Matters seemed to improve when she met John Travis, a builder of whom she became very fond. His mother also liked Eliza, and suggested that she come and clean at the house, a suggestion to which she readily acceded. When she had been employed for a while, Mrs Travis stated that she thought her repentance was genuine and offered her a job as a live-in domestic servant. She gave her blessing to the friendship between Eliza and her son. But Townsend was about to track her

Carlisle Street East.

down once more. She had been at the house for about a fortnight when he arrived to talk to her. Mrs Travis answered the door to him and he asked if Eliza was in. She was upstairs cleaning and Mrs Travis called her down to talk to him. He called out, 'Eliza, your father wants to talk to you.' She came downstairs and they went out into the yard. Mrs Travis closed the door and then approximately ten minutes later she heard the sound of a pistol going off. Opening the door, she was horrified to see the girl coming towards her with her hands thrown up in the air and blood pouring from the front of her dress. The girl staggered towards her and Mrs Travis managed to catch her as she fell through the doorway.

Next she heard the sound of a second shot. A constable named PC James King, who had been patrolling the area, also heard the shot and rushed into the yard where he found Townsend lying on his back. He could immediately see that the man was dead. Townsend was wearing a coat tied up with string and it appeared that he had put the pistol to the front of his chest and fired at close quarters. The wound, which had gone through his coat and his waistcoat, had made a massive hole in the front of his body and his heart and part of his lungs were exposed. The wound was so severe that the constable deduced that he had died immediately. He began to search the yard and found not one but two pistols. They were capable of firing one shot each and there was a quantity of gunpowder and a number of percussion caps in the man's pocket. It seems that he was determined to take both lives. A surgeon was sent for and it was found that Eliza was still alive, although badly wounded. She had been put to bed, where Mr Fotherby, the surgeon, examined her. He found that the bullet had gone through her left side, through her dress and her stays, and she was in great pain. He ordered the body of Townsend to be taken to the neighbouring public house, the Engineers Hotel, where the coroner would hold the inquest the following day. The inquest was duly held, and it seemed to be an open-and-shut case: the jury had no other choice but to bring in a verdict of 'wilful murder' against Townsend. (Although since she was still alive at this point, this seems rather a strange verdict.)

Mr Fotherby attempted to save Eliza, but he knew that it was very unlikely that she would survive. Meanwhile the excitement caused by the crime had spread, and crowds were assembling along the street to view the house and the yard where the crime had happened. Eliza appeared to recover somewhat from her injuries, and for a time it was felt that she might make a recovery. In order to ease the pain, as there was very little in the way of medicine that could be produced to help her, the surgeon bled her on Sunday 15 December and the girl appeared to rally somewhat after this. It was reported that she became more composed. Then, on Tuesday 17 December, eleven days after receiving those terrible injuries, she died a few minutes before 4 a.m. The girl, perhaps because of her youth and beauty, was portrayed by the press as the more innocent party of the two. The reporter stated that:

> Eliza was the victim of her father-in-law's lust and horrible revenge. A man of 40-50 years of age seduced a girl of 16-17 years, a stepdaughter of whom he should be a protector. The birth and death of a child at the beginning of this year publicized to the world the girl's shame. When a young man started to court her she saw a way out of her weary and disgusting past she had made of her life and broke away from her horrid bondage.

The inquest was held in front of the deputy coroner at the Engineers Hotel and it was again agreed that the verdict of wilful murder which had been brought against Townsend was just. Without more details of the case it is hard to make any kind of judgment in this case. We have seen by the great trouble that Townsend had taken that he was determined to kill them both. Had he already threatened that he would kill her, and was she in fear of her life? Had she only found repugnance for her relationship with her ex father-in-law after receiving the attentions of John Travis? We shall never know the answer to these questions. There is no doubt that the case reports lay most of the blame on the older man. We will let the press have the last words on this crime: on his death, it was reported that Townsend's 'self destruction has anticipated the penalty which otherwise the law would have exacted'.

Above: Attercliffe Common, 1790.

Left: Domestic service in Sheffield in 1910.

Chapter Ten

THE JEWEL ROBBERY OF HAYES AND HAWLEY

As we have noted, the policing skills of the Sheffield police force were in their infancy, and great strides in criminal detection were a thing of the future. Crimes were usually solved by the observational skills of the men on the streets of the town. When the villains were arrested and appeared in court, sometimes minimal efforts were used in the defence process, which would of course be unacceptable in the courts of today. This following case underlines not only the observational detective methods of the police force, but also the way in which criminals were dealt with in the justice system of those early Victorian times.

On the night of 9 November 1860, an audacious robbery took place at a Sheffield jeweller's shop. This was similar to a string of robberies which remained unsolved at Rotherham, London and Manchester. It seems that Mr Benjamin Cohen, the jeweller, was in the habit of sleeping at his shop premises on the High Street, Sheffield in order to protect his stock. He usually left the shop at 10.30 p.m. to have his supper before returning to the premises, as was his habit. But on that Friday he had problems closing the large iron door covering the front of the shop and was forced to get some workmen in to attend to it. Finally, about 11 p.m., after locking the back kitchen door with a double bolt, he went to his house in Broomspring Lane (which was just a short distance from his shop). When he returned to his shop premises he found that the back door, which he had previously locked, was open. It was approximately 12.15 a.m. when he returned. He found that eighty watches, both gold and silver, had been taken out of the shop window, as well as some gold rings, pencil cases and other items of jewellery. The back door opened into a small kitchen and sitting room leading into the shop. Realising that his stock had been taken he reported the robbery without further ado to the police station at the Town Hall.

The Chief Constable, Mr Jackson, sent two of his best men to the scene of the crime immediately. These well-known detectives, who figure largely in the capture of thieves and robbers in Victorian Sheffield, were Messrs Robert Airey and Richard Brayshaw. When Mr Cohen reported the robbery they mentioned that two criminals, Thomas Hayes of Rockingham Street (aged thirty-one) and Joseph Hawley of Dyers Hill (aged twenty-six), had been seen in the vicinity of the shop during the last few days.

High Street jeweller's shop, 1890.

The two detectives were aided in their duties by a man called Crabtree, who seemed to be in the habit of accompanying the detectives on their rounds. He was a butcher of Waingate. The detectives had pointed out Hawley and Hayes to him and he had seen the two criminals standing opposite Mr Cohen's shop on 5 November; the three men observed Hayes and Hawley's suspicious activities at the High Street, and saw them once again on the 7th and the 8th of November. When Mr Cohen was having trouble with the iron door, a crowd collected to watch the workmen and the two men were spotted in the crowd. Both men later were found in Duke Street at 1 a.m. in the company of another man. They tried to hide, but the two detectives and their companion spotted them immediately. The third man got away but the two robbers were arrested. In the possession of Hawley was a skeleton key and in the possession of Hayes was an ordinary house key.

The two men were detained at the Town Hall and the detectives went to the house of Hayes' mother, named as Hannah Pears, aged sixty-eight, who had recently rented a cottage at Shale's Yard in Duke Street. They knocked on the door and she appeared at the upstairs window; they demanded entry. She agreed to come downstairs and

Rockingham Street in 1991.

Waingate.

unlock the front door, but as she appeared to be taking her time the two detectives selected the door key found in the possession of Hayes and proceeded to enter the house and to search it. Using only a candle they searched the premises minutely, finding the booty in a plant pot of a downstairs room. The old woman, who was found in bed but fully dressed, was then taken into custody. She told the constable that she had been feeling ill and had warmed some ale for her supper. She went to bed about 11 p.m, and was in bed when she heard Hayes knocking on her door. She went downstairs and saw him at the door; he told her to go to bed. She returned back to bed, but heard two men talking, and then her son called up to her, 'Mother, I shall be back in half an hour. I will take the key with me.' She said that she had then fallen asleep and did not wake up until being aroused by the two detectives. Inside the plant pot they had found a number of gold watches, gold rings and gold pins which were tied up in a handkerchief. These were later identified as belonging to Cohen. The two men had nothing to say when arrested but Hayes had asked that his mother 'be kept out of this' as she knew nothing about the robbery. Hawley remained silent.

They also found that the skeleton key in the possession of Hawley opened the back door of Mr Cohen's shop. The watches and other jewellery were identified by Mr Cohen at between 3 p.m. or 4 p.m. as being his property. Within an hour and a half of being directed by the Chief Constable to take on the case, the thieves

Duke Street, Park, where the thieves were eventually captured.

Shale's Yard, Duke Street.

had been apprehended and the property returned by these two diligent, shrewd detectives. It seems that their methods were exhaustive: when they noticed the two men lurking in the vicinity of the shop on more than one occasion they had made enquiries about them, and discovered the places where they would visit, understanding that if they committed a crime they could be picked up more easily. Amongst other things, they found that Hawley lived with his mother at a house on Dyers Hill. They noted the public houses they frequented and the associates they might find refuge with. When they caught the thieves empty-handed in the vicinity of Duke Street, they deduced that they had lodged the stolen goods at the house of Hayes' mother. It was felt that Hayes told his mother to go back to bed to ensure that she did not witness where the goods were being hidden.

The two prisoners and Hannah Pears were brought before the magistrate, Wm. Smith Esq, on Saturday 10 November 1860, where they were remanded for five days. The following Wednesday, 14 November, they were once more brought before the same magistrate. The men were found guilty of 'burglariously entering the premises of Benjamin Cohen and stealing goods to the value of £500' and committed to take their trial at York. Mrs Pears produced a letter containing a character witness from a Mr Bassett, a metal dealer of Birmingham who had known her for years as a respectable person. He said that Mrs Pears had kept a beerhouse near to his place of business for many years and lived near him in an adjoining street. He had always found her to be an honest and well-meaning woman. The old lady was discharged but she was bound over to appear as a witness against the male prisoners at the Assizes.

The two men appeared at York Assizes on 22 December 1860, defended by Mr C. Foster for Hawley and Mr Price for Hayes. It was noted that the trial was very short as there was much pressing business for the judges to deal with. Indeed, it was reported that, 'Mr Price did not address the jury, the case being so clear against the prisoner.'

Mr Foster contended that the only evidence against Hawley was that a skeleton key had been found on his person and the fact that he had been seen in the High Street at night. There was nothing suspicious about that, 'for surely a man had the right to be in the streets'. However, the jury took no time at all to find both men guilty. Hawley, with a previous conviction proved against him, was sentenced to four years' imprisonment, whereas Hayes was sentenced to twelve months. The reporter noted:

> The case was got through in a very hurried manner ... As soon as the prisoners were arraigned the prosecutor was called and his evidence taken very briefly. The other witnesses were not questioned at any length. Mr Price did not examine a single witness. Mr Foster made a very short speech and the case was quickly concluded.

It is interesting from today's perspective to see this case and all its shortcomings. Whilst there was little doubt that the men were guilty, the methods used for the investigation and prosecution would have caused serious questions to be asked in our modern policing and justice system. The man Crabtree was a mystery. Were these two eminent detectives in the habit of taking strangers with them on duty, and pointing out criminals to them? He was not a special constable, it seems, just a would-be detective. The courts of those times were sometimes rather irreverent: there was much laughter in the court during this examination, on one occasion aimed at the detective' 'methods. Mr Smith, the magistrate, and Mr Turner, who appeared for Pears and Hayes, appear to have had something of a double act going when detective Richard Brayshaw gave his evidence in the Sheffield magistrates' court. When Brayshaw described seeing the male prisoners in the High Street at 9.40 p.m., Mr Smith asked him if he had made a memorandum (a note) to that effect. He replied that he had.

Smith: 'Have you the memorandum here?'
Brayshaw: 'No Sir.'
Turner: 'Where did you make it, in your pocket book?'
Brayshaw: 'In my head, sir.' (Laughter)
Turner to Smith: 'Do you wish to examine it?' (Laughter)

The amusement of the court was nothing compared to the serious, unsmiling and hurried trial at the Assizes. It seems that the two prisoners were dispatched efficiently, and certainly in Hayes' instance his defence was extremely limited. Although we still know of miscarriages of justice, and there is little doubt that the two men were not innocent of the crime, this summary dismissal would surely not have gone unchallenged today.

Chapter Eleven

✦ NED THE KAFFIR ✦

Sheffield, like many other towns in Britain in the early nineteenth century, had a very strong anti-slavery movement. One of the main contributors to this was a woman called Mary Anne Rawson. She lived with her parents at Wincobank Hall and she formed the 1827 Sheffield Female Anti-Slavery Society which called for the immediate release of slaves (rather than the gradual release which was the main thrust behind other anti-slavery organisations). She campaigned in Sheffield to ban products such as coffee and sugar which had come from plantations owned by slave owners. She gave lectures and distributed leaflets, and, as a result of this, the sale of such products declined in the town. By 1833 the mood of the nation was changing, due in no small part to the labours of such people as Miss Rawson. That year the Abolition of Slavery Act was passed, outlawing slavery in the British Dominions. By 1839 the British and Foreign Anti-Slavery Society was formed in order to outlaw slavery throughout the world. This society still exists today (as Anti-Slavery International Society). Mary Anne Rawson of Sheffield is one of the few women pictured at the first World Anti-Slavery Society Conference of 1840 in the painting by Benjamin Haydon.

Nevertheless, black servants continued to be a prized possession of the white gentry, and the ownership of these servants gave a status to such owners (as we see in the many portraits of them). Once the anti-slavery law was passed, many kept the servants on as family retainers. One of these families was a that of a Mr Handley, who owned estates in South Africa in Natal and a residence in Blackburn near to Sheffield. In December 1859 he was in Sheffield, and had brought a young servant named as 'Ned' with him on his return to this country. Ned had been involved in the Zulu civil war when the Zulu King Panda had attacked the village where he lived. To escape wholesale massacre he, and a few other survivors, had fled to the British town of Natal. There he had gained employment with a 'respectable' merchant at Pietermaritzburg (the capital of the colony of Natal). After a few years he had begun working for Mr Handley as a servant looking after his two children.

In December 1859, after a stay of three or four months at the estate near Blackburn, it was decided that the family would move back to the estates at Natal. Ned decided that he did not wish to return, so he ran away from the house. He lived wild in the woods around Blackburn from the end of August to the end of

Wincobank Hall, where Mary Anne Rawson lived with her parents in 1820.

October before he was captured. A man called Simmons was walking through the churchyard at 11.30 p.m. on the night of 25 October when he saw a fire; approaching the fire he saw Ned lying on the floor with his feet towards the flames. On seeing him, Ned leapt to his feet and threatened the newcomer with a sharp stick. Simmons hurriedly left and went to fetch the police. Naturally, by the time they returned Ned had gone. At the campsite they found a woman's dress, a scythe and pieces of shoulder and leg of cooked mutton. The Sheffield Police authorities eventually captured him and took him to the police station based at Eckington on the border of North-East Derbyshire. There they found that the young man could not speak any English, nor understand what was being said to him. As a result of this the police authorities felt that it would be useless to try him for sheep stealing, and the charges were dropped.

His master had by now gone back to Natal. A man named Brady from Rotherham contacted the Anti-Slavery Society in Sheffield as Ned was thought to be a runaway slave, but when they contacted him a Mr Chameroozon, a fellow South African, spoke to the police authorities. He also spoke to Mr Handley, who demanded that Ned be returned to him forthwith. The South African pointed out that since the Abolition of Slavery Act, to remove him from England without his consent would be most unwise. He stated that under the terms of the Act, 'it would render it most dangerous for a British subject to own a slave'. The matter was considered closed when Mr Handley paid Ned the £11 owed to him in wages, thereby proving that Ned was a servant and not a slave. Mr Chameroozon suggested that Ned be sent to London to the Strangers' House on the West India Dock Road, run by Colonel Hughes, where it was hoped they would find someone who could converse with him. In an act of great generosity, a subscription was started for him by Mr T. Need Esq., who was one of the justices on the Eckington bench, and it was agreed that he would be taken to London and placed under the protection of the British and Foreign Anti-Slavery Society in London. In order to make sure that he arrived safely, Superintendent Chawner of Eckingham accompanied him on his journey.

His journey to the big city, however, was not a resolution to the problem, as in the few weeks he was there he ran away from the Strangers' House on three different occasions: the last time resulted in his capture a week later in Highgate Woods. The reporter for the *Rotherham and Masbrough Advertiser* noted that 'he failed to settle to civilized life'. He was captured after once again being driven by hunger to steal a sheep, and the authorities were once more unsure what should be done with him due to his inability to speak English. The newspaper reports drew the attention of a South African pioneer of Natal who offered his services as interpreter. He was the Hon. Jonas Bergtheil Esq., who had gone to South Africa in 1844, where he settled among the Boers as a farmer, and was a member of the Council of Natal. He encouraged British people to emigrate to South Africa and in 1847 he headed a group of forty families who went out to that country in search of a better life. He periodically came back to England and it was on one of these visits that he heard the sad story of Ned. He went to the Clerkenwell House of Correction (where Ned was being held on remand until the authorities could decide what to do with him) and recognised Ned as a Zulu – unmistakable, he claimed, for their height and dignity. In fact, he recognised him as a servant of Mr Handley as he had met him at Greytown, a seaport of Durban, when Mr Handley was setting off for his return to Sheffield. Finally being able to converse in his own language, Ned told him about the horrendous journey to England: he had suffered so badly from seasickness that he was determined not to undertake another journey by sea. He described his days in hiding at Sheffield and London and how he was forced to kill sheep to survive. He spoke about being surprised not to have been punished for stealing the sheep in Sheffield, as he would surely have been punished in his own country.

Mr Bergthiel was sympathetic to his story and announced that Ned would be prepared to work for any man in England providing he did not have to go to sea again. Before anything could be done, however – now thankfully with a translator in tow – he was brought to the Highgate magistrates on 3 December 1859 charged with 'killing a sheep, the property of George Fletcher and feloniously stealing the carcass to the value of £2 10s'. At this court the magistrates read out a letter to the jury from Mr Chameroozon describing his earlier life. The following extract comes from that letter:

> He is a Zulu Kaffir. He is quite uncivilized and although saying he wants to stay in the country and work it is clear to me that he would not be able to live under the restraints of civilized life, but would take the first opportunity to take to the woods and resume in England the life of a Kaffir.

Mr Bergthiel had written a letter to the *London Telegraph* outlining Ned's story. It seems that the reason he had run away so many times from the Strangers' House was that every person who came to see him there mentioned a return to Natal, and he was fearful of being made to return by sea. He told the Hon. Bergthiel that he was astonished that in this country instead of being punished for stealing sheep he was taken to London to live in a very comfortable house. Bergthiel advocated for Ned and asked the magistrates to deal leniently with him, and not send him to prison where he would have to mix with the more criminal members of society. The law, however, had to take its course, and he was sent for trial at Newgate. We unfortunately have no more information on Ned, but it is to be hoped that he did not suffer the traditional punishment for sheep stealing – death by hanging.

Chapter Twelve

'A DISGUSTING CASE'

In a city as big as Sheffield there were many reports of immorality, many of which would undoubtedly be reported widely in the local newspapers. One would have thought that hardened hacks would have been used to tales of couples and their sexual indiscretions, but the reporter from the *Sheffield and Rotherham Independent*, it seems, was particularly scandalised by the following case. In fact, the title of this chapter is taken from his byline: 'A disgusting case.'

On Monday 15 February 1865, a couple who had spent the weekend together went into the Cock Inn, Wicker. He was Joseph Bellamy, who was married with four children, and she was Mary Bailey, the wife of Isaac Bailey. It seems that they had met by appointment on Saturday 12 February at the Royal Hotel and had spent the rest of the weekend sleeping and drinking. Meanwhile, a frantic Mrs Bellamy called at the Town Hall to report that her husband had gone missing. In such circumstances the police would have been unable to do much about the situation (apart from suggest Bellamy go back to his wife). The couple were reportedly 'fresh' [drunk] when they arrived at the Cock Inn. Thomas Morrison, the landlord of the inn, was also living with a woman and her name was Emma Ward. It seems that there were a lot of arguments between the pair: in fact, Bailey had intervened twice in arguments between Morrison and Ward during the evening of the 15th, and Morrison had resented her interference on both occasions – and had told her so in no uncertain terms. Despite the arguments, it seems that Morrison gave permission for the couple to sleep on the sofa in one of the 'low rooms' (but was in reality a kitchen which belonged to the Cock Inn). They got up on Tuesday at about 11 a.m. and proceeded to drink for the rest of the day until 1 a.m. or 2 a.m. on Wednesday morning, with George Cutts of Lambert Street as a companion.

Before they were able to go to bed, yet another argument broke out between Morrison and Ward up in the bedroom. By now all four of them had been drinking steadily, and none of them were sober. Bellamy said that although he could hear the couple arguing, he did not hear any sounds of scuffling, but only words (although he later agreed that he could not make out the conversation). Once more Bailey said

Royal Hotel, Waingate where Joseph Bellamy and Mary Bailey spent the weekend of 2 February 1865.

that she would try to calm the situation down, and up she went to the bedroom that the couple shared. Bellamy waited for a while. When she did not return after ten to fifteen minutes, he went upstairs to find her lying on the bed with Morrison trying to loosen her clothing. At the side of Morrison was Ward, who was very drunk and had passed out. Bellamy noted that Bailey had blood coming out of her ear and he asked Morrison, 'Good God – whatever is the matter?'

'She has fallen downstairs,' he replied.

'It is a curious thing that I did not hear her,' he replied.

Morrison just repeated what he had said before – that she had fallen downstairs. Bellamy asked if he should call a doctor, as the woman was now bleeding profusely from the ear, but Morrison told Bellamy that she would be all right, providing she had some sleep. Bellamy agreed to stay with her and sat by the bed for most of the night. Still reluctant to call in a surgeon, about 6 a.m. he went to fetch a woman from the bottom of Carver Street. She had a look at Bailey and agreed with Morrison that she would be 'better when she had some sleep'. Ward was at this time still described as insensible.

Later that morning, George Cutts went back to the Cock Inn. Morrison and Ward were there and Morrison told him that Bailey had fallen down the stairs and hurt herself very badly the previous night. (Bellamy had by now fled the scene, no doubt going back to his wife.) Morrison took Cutts to see the insensible woman and he was very alarmed when he saw the state that she was in. He told Morrison to send for a surgeon as soon as possible. Still the couple did nothing to help the injured woman. Thomas Kay Thompson (was this the same man as in Death at the Mail Coach Inn?) arrived at the inn at 11 a.m. and he was also told about the accident the previous evening. Another (unnamed) woman went upstairs to look at Bailey, and told the other people at the inn that she was worse. Finally Thompson went up to look at her. Morrison and Ward were fearful of bringing a surgeon to the house, so they decided that they would take her to her sister's house instead, where they hoped she could be cared for. Morrison agreed to pay for the cab and Bailey, who was still insensible, was bundled into it accompanied by Ward. She was taken to the home of her sister Hannah Jarvis on Wednesday and she died the following Monday 21 February. Bailey never regained consciousness, nor did she speak during the time she was at her sister's house.

Mr Edwin Richardson was called to see her the following day and he realised that her condition was very poor. He consulted Mr John Shaw, a surgeon of Attercliffe, and they both agreed that she was labouring under a compression of the brain caused by a fracture of the skull. She had several bruises. The right elbow was black and there was considerable injury to her right hip and on the right side of her neck. Mr Richardson visited her daily until her death on the Monday. That same evening he and Mr Shaw undertook the post mortem at the request of the coroner and Ward and Morrison were arrested and charged with manslaughter.

One of the courts on Lambert Street.

The inquest was held on Tuesday 22 February at the White Hart Inn, Church Street, Attercliffe, in front of the coroner, Mr Badger. Both surgeons were the first to give evidence, Mr Richardson stating that when he first examined the deceased she was unconscious. He had seen her every day up to her death. He was unsure what the nature of her injuries were at this point but the post mortem had indicated that she had died from effusion of blood on the brain caused by an extensive fracture of the skull, though he could not say whether that fracture had been caused by a blow or a fall. Mr Shaw told the coroner that he agreed with his colleague on his diagnosis and described how, when the skull cap was removed, the membranes of the deceased's brain were 'much congested' and there was a large quantity of coagulation of the blood covering the whole left hemisphere of the brain. He gave his opinion that the cause of death was from a heavy fall and not from a blow.

The evidence from Bellamy, Morrison and Ward was listened to with great interest: whilst they were in the dock the court was totally silent. Bellamy denied that he had had anything to drink at all during the night's events, but Morrison, who listed all the drinks that he had served him during that night, disproved this. He showed the coroner that the couple had consumed thirteen pints of ale as well as drinks of rum and gin, and showed the list to the coroner and the jury. Bellamy described the events of the night and spoke to the jury about finding Bailey upstairs. One of the jurymen asked him if there were any weapons in the bedroom, but he told him that there weren't. He told the coroner that there were two doors in between the kitchen and the stairs and it was possible that he had not heard her fall or call out to him. He described Bailey as being very drunk as she had not had much to eat, but 'she knew what she was doing'. He stated, 'I cannot swear that she did not fall downstairs nor can I charge Morrison with having thrown her down.' However, he did concede that he had no idea how Morrison had got her back up the stairs alone – or why he had not called out for Bellamy to help him.

Morrison next took the stand and told the coroner that when he went to bed it was between 1 a.m. and 2 p.m. He was undressing, he said, when he heard Bailey fall down the stairs. He saw her at the bottom of the stairs and he picked her up and carried her up to the bedroom. He stated that he had not asked Bellamy to help him, as he was 'too fresh'. He said that Bellamy had got into bed with the two women and that he had slept on the sofa in the kitchen instead. (Bellamy was recalled and denied climbing into bed with the two women.) The female prisoner, Emma Ward, gave evidence and she told the coroner that she had been married to a man named George Walker from whom she was now separated. She had lived with Morrison for about three weeks. She said she had been drinking with him on the Tuesday night, but then an argument had broken out where he told her to get out of his sight; she claimed that she had gone to bed to be out of his way, admitting that she was quite drunk. She said that she woke about 7 a.m. and found Bailey in bed at the side of her and had tried to rouse her. Bailey had said to her, 'let me be a bit'. She went downstairs and asked Morrison what had happened and he told her that Bailey had fallen down the stairs and that he and Bellamy had carried her up the stairs and put her into bed. Ward stated that she had no knowledge of what had happened and had only found the woman at the side of her when she awoke.

The coroner, summing up for the jury, could not contain his repugnance for the behaviour exhibited by the four protagonists. The reporter stated that: 'He spoke to them in very severe terms of the conduct of the persons connected with this affair especially reproving Bellamy and Morrison for the disgraceful manner of their lives.' The coroner told the jury that the evidence was not sufficient to justify them in admitting the prisoners, intimating his impression that the deceased's injuries had been caused by her falling downstairs. The jury, after a short consultation, returned the verdict that death had resulted from the injuries as stated in the medical evidence, but how those injuries were received there was no evidence to show. The prisoners were detained in custody, and taken in front of the magistrate, T. Dann Esq, the following morning. Ward was severely reprimanded for her part in this death and discharged. Morrison was ordered to enter into his own recognisances of £20 for his future good behaviour and to pay the court costs.

The case indicates the profligate lives that many people led in the town of Sheffield; alcohol was, for many, their only escape. The fact that all of the parties were very drunk makes it hard to come to any conclusion other than the one reached by the jury.

Chapter Thirteen

✴ AN AUDACIOUS THIEF ✴

Employers during the Victorian era, bereft of the technology we have today, had to take much of what their employees told them on trust. William Moore Walters tried to fool his employer by emphasising his religious qualities, hoping that this would make his employer trust him. It seemed to work, and in February 1860 he was given money and cheques to pay into the bank whilst his employer went for lunch. Walters of Granville Street, Park was employed as a clerk by Messrs Bassett & Lodge, wholesale confectioners of Portland Street, Sheffield. (George Bassett went on to form the family firm of Bassett's and in 1890 created Bassett's Liquorice Allsorts, for which they became famous.) Moore had only been employed by them as bookkeeper for two months and was frequently trusted to take money to the bank. At lunchtime of Friday 27 January 1860, he was ordered by Mr Bassett to take £250 to the Union bank. The amount consisted of £90 in cash and the remainder in Bank of England and local notes and cheques. When he returned from his lunch, Mr Bassett asked him for the bankbook and he told him that the bank had retained it in order to enter the transaction. This had happened before and so Bassett was not duly alarmed. Walters remained at his post until 7.30 p.m. on Friday without any suspicion being cast upon him. On Saturday, Mr Bassett received the most impudent letter, which read:

January 27th 1860

Mr Bassett

Dear Sir. You will be surprised instead of seeing me as usual to receive this communication. I had an offer on Thursday to go out to Valparaiso and the remuneration was so good that the prospects have tempted me to borrow from you the cash to start with. Nay, sir, do not be too hasty in your judgment, I have but borrowed it and I swear and vow to you, as I hope for prosperity in this life and happiness in that to come, you shall have every farthing of your money back within 12 months and interest at 6% six months after. I know that you will not, cannot under the circumstances believe it, but if you shall wait time will prove it. You will be at a loss to understand the meaning of all this but when I have cleared my conscience by returning to you that which is yours, you will not sympathise but pity me. As fervently and truly as I have vowed to return you the loan, so truly do I swear never to be brought to face any shame should you send after me, nay as fearful as the act may be, I would plunge my soul unprepared to The Judge than to be taken to face an earthly tribunal. O Sir if you can spare for 12 months the use of a few pounds to start a fellow creature in this life, look upon this as a loan and let it not go forth that I am a robber, swindler, thief. I can say no more at present, but on the 1st March you shall receive an installment and on the 1st of each month further installments until it is all paid off.

Farewell

W. Walters

There followed a written account of the money borrowed, and the total amount (discounting his wages). Walters was a married man with two children and made a great show of being a very religious man – on the surface. He was a leader at prayer meetings, attended Bible classes and was a Sunday school teacher. But his diary recorded a very different man, one who ill-treated his wife, led an immoral life and indulged in liaisons with other women, described as 'not of a respectable character'. On the same day as he sent the above letter, he wrote a note to his wife telling quite a different story. He wrote to her:

Saturday morning

Dear Jane –

By the time you receive this I shall be on my way to America. I have had an excellent chance offered to me and have accepted it. I shall leave England early next week. I could not tell you about it for many reasons. Mr Bassett has lent me the cash to proceed with. I advise you to sell what you can and go and live at home until I send for you. I can say no more now, when I arrive safe there I will write to you all the particulars.

Yours William.

Kiss the children. Goodbye.

Just to keep her until he saw her again he enclosed a £5 note in the letter. During the previous day he had, without raising her suspicions, obtained as much money as there was in the house. It appears that Walters had not been to the bank at all. Finding the cheques and notes, she returned them to Mr Bassett along with the bankbook and the £5 note which Walters had left her. A description of Walters followed, describing him as being '27 years of age, five foot seven or eight inches high, pale complexion, small sandy whiskers, light curly hair, large prominent blue eyes, round shoulders, rather knock kneed, stoops a little, treads heavily on heels when walking and turns his toes out.'

Granville Street, Park.

He generally, it was said, 'speaks quickly' and when excited had a slight impediment in his speech. He was last seen 'wearing a brown cloth, close fitting overcoat with a velvet collar and new strong boots which had brass eyelet holes up the front'.

The following week, the story got more intriguing. A woman employed in the warehouse of Bassett & Lodge named Mary Jackson, aged eighteen, to whom Walters had been paying attention, also received a letter from him stating that he loved her above all others and could not love anyone else. Miss Jackson had become friendly with another man, described as William L., whom Walters had told that he was 'just friends' with Miss Jackson. William L. warned her that 'he was a fine jackdaw that you have taken up with. But remember that all that glitters is not gold'. Indeed her parents, unaware that Walters was married, allowed him to sit with her until eleven o'clock on the evening before he absconded. Walters, in his letter to her, stated that he was enclosing two letters and that she was to send whichever one showed her true feelings for him. He enclosed two envelopes, both addressed to William Moore at General Post Office, London – to be called for. One stated: 'I will be true and faithful to you'; the other, 'you have lost my heart and affections'. Declaring his love, he wrote that he would come for her in four years time and asked her to wait for him.

The letter and its enclosures were handed to Mr Bassett, who took them to the Chief Constable of Sheffield, Mr Jackson. Miss Jackson (no relation), who by now must have been rather confused by events, had not written back to Walters and she received another letter begging her not to keep him in suspense any longer but to send one of the two letter to him in London. He wrote passionately:

I swear by heaven, by the hope I have of getting there that I will be faithful until death. I love none none NONE but you. I am mad with despair, have compassion and let me hear from you. Until I do I shall be a most unhappy man, but still your faithful and devoted William.

The Chief Constable dispatched Detective Airey to London after him on 3 February. Mr Bassett accompanied the detective and, following the dispatch of the letter that Walters would find most agreeable, they were successful in capturing him – he arrived in person to collect it. He did not suspect the letter would have fallen into any other hands than Miss Jackson's, and so when he arrived at the post office at 10.30 a.m. on Saturday morning to collect the letter, they captured him.

They had found a position where they could observe the post office without him seeing them, and could not believe their luck when they spotted him coming towards them. In order to disguise himself, he had shaven off his beard and made his naturally curly hair straight; he was wearing what was described as a 'glazed cap' and an Inverness cape rather than the clothes he had been described as wearing when he left Sheffield. Airey seized him by both arms, booming 'How do you do, Mr Walters? I am from Sheffield!' before he had time to ask the clerk anything. Walters was so taken aback that he fell back as if paralysed. Placing him in a cab they proceeded on the journey back to Sheffield. He asked if he could be tried in London and appeared to be despondent at the thought of returning to Sheffield and having to face people there. A few moments later Detective Airey, noting that his countenance had changed somewhat, saw him slip his right hand into his pocket and he grabbed his hand to stop him. The detective found a pistol in the pocket, loaded and primed to shoot. Detective Airey then searched him and found a second pistol in the same condition. They took him to a police station where, searching him more thoroughly, they found a gold watch, a guard and a gold pin, and the £55 16s 2d remaining from the stolen money, together with several articles which he had bought. Detective Airey asked him where he had lodged whilst in London, and he told him that he had been staying at No. 21 St Mays Building, St Martin's Lane. He was then charged, and he declared that he was sorry for what he had done.

When his lodgings were searched the police found a smart travelling trunk, a new desk containing a number of letters, and a diary, which catalogued his travels since he had left Sheffield. He listed his visits to Miss Jackson ending on the day he absconded – taking his opportunity as his wife had gone to Birmingham. On the 27th he wrote, 'detained cash, £90'. On the morning of the 26th, he left Sheffield for Doncaster and he recorded the fare as being 1*s* 7*d*. At Doncaster he bought a shirt, hat and neckties amounting to £1 9*s* 11*d*. He left Doncaster the same day and went to Leeds, where he stayed at the Beescroft Hotel and where he purchased two pistols for 10*s*, powder, shot and a pouch. Described by the reporter as 'chapel-going hypocrisy', he lists 'Leeds, chapel in the evening'. They also found a bottle of poison at the side of his bed, proving that he was prepared to do away with himself rather than be taken into custody. They also found that although he had boasted about going to America, he had placed advertisements offering £5 to anyone prepared to offer him some employment. The police discovered that one such advertisement

Distribution of soup at Brightside in 1870.

was returned by *The Times*, who stated that it was against their policy to allow advertisers to offer inducements as a way of procuring situations or appointments.

Walters was brought before the magistrates at Sheffield on 11 February 1860. The prisoner appeared to have lost all his spirit, and hung his head with shame when ordered by the magistrate to go to trial at the Sheffield Sessions on 2 March. He told the judge that he asked for mercy: that he had not intended to defraud Mr Bassett, but when he finally 'left prison homeless, friendless and a penniless wanderer' he still intended to pay back the amount in full. The judge told him in response that his was the largest robbery that had come to his notice and that even though it was a first offence, the court would pronounce a heavier sentence than is usual: he sentenced him to serve twelve calendar months with hard labour in the Wakefield House of Correction.

This case sums up the chronicles of crime in Sheffield during the Victorian period. I hope readers have found it a snapshot of the lives of the more disreputable types of criminals of the town. Life was difficult for Sheffield's poor, and many crimes were committed to fend off starvation. Just ten years after the above crime, a soup kitchen was opened in Brightside, where there was much poverty due to industrial distress. I think this selection also shows, however, that there were many determined criminals in the area, men (and women) who committed crime for gain and would oppose anyone who stood in their way. Sheffield today is a bustling city which attracts shoppers, tourists and academics alike, and thankfully we can now travel into and out of the city in safety.

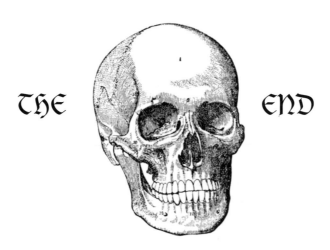

THE END

Other titles published by The History Press

Murder and Crime in Rotherham
MARGARET DRINKALL

This absorbing collection of some of the foulest deeds from Rotherham's past promises to interest anyone who is unaware of this forgotten part of the town's character. With stories ranging from child murders to brutal stabbings, the misdemeanours that are revealed promise to shock and fascinate in equal measure. Illustrated with both rare images and archive reports, this volume shows just how difficult life in Victorian England was for those who had nowhere else to turn.

978 0 7524 5424 5

Murder and Crime in Sheffield
MARGARET DRINKALL

The grim and bloody events in this book, many of which have not been written about for more than a century, reveal the dark heart of Victorian Yorkshire. Some of these gruesome tales would not look out of place in a work of fiction – a body abandoned in the middle of the street, a man murdered by his wife and her lover and a daring case of highway robbery. Richly illustrated with archive and modern photographs, it will fascinate anyone with an interest in Sheffield's dark past.

978 07 524 5568 6

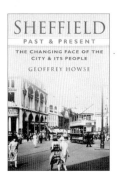

Sheffield Past & Present: The Changing Face of the City & its People
GEOFFREY HOWSE

Sheffield Past & Present gives a fascinating insight into the dramatic changes that have taken place in the city during the twentieth century: changing types of transport and fashion, the developing character of streets and districts as they took on the form that is familiar today. The astonishing periods of growth that occurred during the late Victorian and Edwardian eras, and since the Second World War, are particularly well illustrated. The author has combined a remarkable selection of archive photographs with modern views of the same scenes.

978 0 7509 4895 1

Dickens' Dreadful Almanac: A Terrible Event for Every Day of the Year
EDITED BY CATE LUDLOW

In amongst the pages of Dickens' monthly supplement to *Household Words*, a very strange and very British history lurks. Under the headings of 'Narrative of Law and Crime' and 'Narrative of Accident and Disaster' may be found an astonishing catalogue of terrible, grisly and most dreadful Victorian events. With a terrifying true tale for every day of the year, *Dickens' Dreadful Almanac* will delight lovers of his work everywhere.

978 0 7524 5828 1

Visit our website and discover thousands of other History Press books.

www.thehistorypress.co.uk